SMALL
BUSINESS IN
TOUGH TIMES

SMALL BUSINESS IN TOUGH TIMES

HOW TO SURVIVE AND PROSPER

John Day

Pfeiffer & COMPANY

Amsterdam • Johannesburg • London
San Diego • Sydney • Toronto

Pfeiffer & Company
8517 Production Avenue
San Diego, CA 92121-2280

Page Compositor: Terry Journey

Cover: Tom Lewis, Inc.

ISBN: 0-89384-242-7

Printed in the United States of America

Printing 1 2 3 4 5 6 7 8 9 10

CONTENTS

PREFACE

In this book I use the word *entrepreneur* to describe the person who goes into business to make something out of nothing and to take on and win the challenge of financial independence in a materialistic society. Most people are not fully aware of the risk taking, courage, and daring required to be a successful entrepreneur.

Thanks to the media's quest for "scoops," much of the business news that reaches the wider population is not only negative but also pertains to big business only. Except in the better-quality financial press, the small business story has for too long been overlooked in the rush for sensational coverage.

Stories about small business are invariably stories about people like you and me, stories about both success and failure. As such, they are always interesting. I have included some of them here, trusting that they will inform, challenge, warn, encourage, reassure, or inspire readers.

There are three phases in a business career: getting there, being there, and staying there. In particularly tough times, a fourth phase is introduced: getting out. The four parts of this book deal with these phases. Even if you have already made it in business and are tempted to go straight to Part Three, I urge you to read the first two parts as well. Like a human life, in which childhood events have a profound influence on adulthood, a business career is set in the early stages of its development. Thus, a reexamination of your past business activities might throw light on your present and your future prospects. Unlike a human life, though, a business career can have any number of comebacks; and some of the comments, advice, and anecdotes offered in Parts One and Two might prompt you to do things differently in your next business, should you find yourself starting all over again.

John Day

FOREWORD

In the past several years, there has been a higher than usual casualty rate among small businesses. It is important to understand why this has happened. When you study John Day's book you will see that he places a great deal of emphasis on the preparation of the business plan and on monitoring the money that is coming in, that is likely to come in, and that is likely to go out.

Recessions always take a toll on small and large businesses that are highly leveraged because their forecasts are overly optimistic. This time around there has been an additional element. Many of the casualties effectively mortgaged their profits by borrowing money to invest in the real estate market, using negative financing to reduce tax payments. Had they worked with a carefully prepared plan to concentrate their capital and effort on the businesses they had chosen, more might have survived the crunch and now be in a position to prosper. Banks that loaned money to these businesses in the belief that property would hold its value have been "taken to the cleaners" with these businesses. As a result, banks had many of their best executives collecting debts and managing problem accounts.

The experiences of the past will dissuade many people from starting their own businesses and tend to make bankers nervous. But in time common sense will prevail—particularly as many former executives of large corporations look to establish new lives now that big companies no longer offer job security.

Remember that banks receive small margins from transactions with large corporations. The most profitable business for banks, outside the housing market, is sound loans to smaller enterprises, and so the position for small businesses will surely improve. During the coming decade, ways to provide equity capital for the better small enterprises will increase. Smaller businesses are major employers of labor because they usually use it far more efficiently than large corporations with layers of management.

The coming years will see opportunities for smaller enterprises increase generally. Not only will more government work be contracted out to more efficient smaller groups, but larger corporations will turn to smaller enterprises to undertake certain functions. (The giant McDonald's Corporation franchises its stores rather than operate them itself. And one of the secrets of the Japanese success in the motor vehicle industry is the large network of smaller component manufacturers that are aided by communal computer and other developmental facilities.) So don't despair if life is tough at the moment; the future is on your side if your business or your plan is good.

As you face this time of optimism, I commend John Day's book to you.

Robert Gottliebsen
Chairman and Editorial Director
Business Review Weekly Publications

INTRODUCTION

It is not easy to define small business. A small business can be a one-person band or a concern employing a hundred people. A business is deemed "small" if it is independently owned and operated and is not dominant in its field of operation. For the purposes of this book, a business is considered "small" if it is not big enough to employ its own financial expert.

Operating a small business in tough times should be the same as operating a small business in easy times: It is always a challenge and a struggle. But there is nothing like an economic recession to remind all players of the golden rules on which every commercial enterprise should be built. It is interesting that many of the entrepreneurs who flourish in easy times, and make a great show of their gains, are the first to go under in tough times; while many middle-of-the-road, low-profile operators manage to pull through with hardly a waver in their profits. The reason for this is simply that the basic principles of successful business are perennial—they never change.

In some ways, the crisis point brought about by adverse conditions beyond their control is a blessing in disguise for small business operators, because it forces them to appreciate firsthand the grounds on which these principles are built. Lessons learned through personal failure always hit harder than abstract ones. And where there is pain there is an incentive to avoid a repetition of the experience that caused that pain. This book will therefore be of value to all people who operate, or want to operate, a small business—in tough times, in all times.

Apart from the enduring principles that underlie business success, there are some measures that can be used to cope in emergencies. These serve as first-aid only and should not take precedence over longer term priorities. They might involve changing the schedule and sequence of planned business activities, perhaps a shifting emphasis from one area to another, or suspending or delaying development plans. Whatever means is chosen to overcome an immediate crisis, it should be remembered that the economy moves in cycles. Sooner or later tough times will become easier times; and once the good times have returned they will eventually fade into bad again. Basically, the two sets of conditions are at opposite ends of a spectrum, and the pendulum of economic cycles swings between them. Because the one extreme causes the other, each can be used to prepare for the other.

Ups and downs in the economy might also be seen as mountains and valleys: Rather than stare gloomily into the abyss, small business operators should fix one eye on the other side and brace themselves for the crossing. By treating all problems as learning experiences, small business operators can reinvest their enhanced knowledge in their own futures, thereby turning negative situations to their ultimate advantage. In tough times the immediate priority is to survive — survive this crisis in order to prosper in the future.

PART ONE

GETTING THERE

1

THE PERSON BEHIND THE BUSINESS

The Enterprising Type

It is interesting to ask self-employed people what made them leave the security of a good job to strike out on their own. Most say they did so to escape from unemployment, actual or anticipated; to establish sources of supplementary income; or to be their own bosses. Some say they are basically insecure and must prove their worth on their own. Others claim that they are bored by the slow pace in a large company and hunger for more action. Others even say that they were motivated by a nagging spouse, by a desire to keep up with the Joneses, or by a hero in business. (Discover the identity of an entrepreneur's hero and you will learn a lot about him or her.)

If money ever enters the picture, it is usually in the form of the rhetorical question, "Why should I get only 15 percent of the revenue I am earning when I could get 100 percent?" Only very few self-employed people describe themselves as capitalists in the traditional sense of hoping to accumulate substantial profits. Although, by definition, the achievement of wealth must be the ultimate aim of any entrepreneur, a fascination with the process of *getting there* is a more common motivating factor.

The typical entrepreneur is a strong individualist and a born optimist. To him or her the bucket is not half empty but half full. This trait is sometimes taken to excess, but surviving the false starts, near failures, and disappointments that entrepreneurs face every day does, indeed, require undying optimism. The entrepreneur sees solutions, not problems, and finds opportunities where others might find despair.

> **Case Study.** Jim is a fellow who grew up in a businesslike family and was destined to be enterprising. He is the epitome of an entrepreneur. He sleeps no more than six hours a night. In the mornings he reads every available newspaper, clips articles, and files everything according to subject headings. He calls himself a public relations man. Jim is into contacts; he knows all the "right" people—not because of his family, but because he makes an effort to meet such people. He joins the "right" clubs. He is always building, looking for ideas, looking for opportunities.
>
> At the beginning of the current economic downturn, rather than grumble, Jim went out and borrowed four or five books about earlier depressions to look for opportunities to make some money. He concluded that the number of poor people was likely to increase and, given that the cheapest nutritional meal is fish, he set up a business supplying fish to the Salvation Army.

A popular misconception is that the entrepreneur is willing to accept risks and to gamble. In fact, most entrepreneurs are not as inclined to take risks as many people would think. Rather than back the ten-to-one shot, they tend to go for the three-to-one shot. Whether at leisure or in business, successful entrepreneurs set themselves exciting but realistic goals, which they attain or exceed.

Self-employment gives you freedom of choice. You work in the area that appeals to you and devote as many hours as you wish to your business and to the execution of your ideas. One of the main reasons people go into their own businesses is so that they can be justly rewarded for their efforts, skill, and expertise. But since the rewards may be a long time coming, patience and perseverance are required.

Admittedly, the self-employed face more uncertainty than people who remain in paid employment, but in hard times neither their jobs nor their employers' survival is guaranteed.

> **Case Study.** Brian, a very competent accountant, recently relocated to the country to work for a new company. He put his heart and soul into his job, living in a trailer for many months away from his family, and finally buying a home in the town where he worked. The very day his family was moving, his wife was killed in a car accident. Less than six months later the business was sold and Brian, then aged 55, was laid off. Where could he go?

The uncertainty of self-employment simply means that you need to have a strong ego, that you cannot afford to be easily discouraged, that you must forge on without stopping to justify yourself. To try and to fail is better than not to try at all.

To prosper in your own business you must be honest, especially with yourself, and be able to enjoy your undertaking, make it work *for*, not *against* you. Above all, you must have plenty of self-discipline—discipline to adhere to your plans, honor your commitments, work the required hours, and produce a quality product on time and at the quoted price. You must take pride in your efforts. In a small business, just as in a sport, a true champion is never satisfied and is always developing the competitive instinct to continue to strive, to achieve greater goals.

Setting up and running your own business, and managing to survive, is the ultimate test of whether you are the enterprising type. You make the decisions and you are responsible only to yourself. If the business succeeds, the resulting pride and satisfaction are yours alone; if it fails, only you can be blamed.

> **Case Study.** Paul wanted to set up a retail clothing business. For many years he had worked for well-known companies. He had progressed from buying to marketing to retail sales and did stints in account collections and credit card sales. In other words, he had a fairly well-grounded career. At the age of twenty-six he had little money and no experience in running a small business. What he did have were apparently innate enterprising characteristics. He embarked on a number of courses, read lots of books, and did some feasibility studies. From his experience with the larger chains, he knew all about markups and was in touch with the relevant suppliers and buyers of clothing. He set about doing his business plan.
>
> Paul needed much less sleep than the average person. In the first twelve months of setting up his business, he was constantly making notes. When questioned about this he said, "While my mind's working, while I am being productive, I can concentrate. As things come to mind, I document them. I don't want to take the subordinate or the lazy attitude of the nine-to-fiver. I am going to concentrate on making this business successful."
>
> Three years later Paul's business is successful. He has opened up two new menswear shops under his own label. He enjoys good profits and now has a little more time to himself, but when required he still rolls up his sleeves.

Born to Do Business?

It is sometimes said that someone was "born to be in business." It is certainly true that to be successful in business you have to be able to cope with stress, frustration, disappointment, and other intellectual as well as physical rigors. Any hereditary factor or childhood conditioning that fosters such traits will therefore assist in coping.

The successful entrepreneur tends to have had relevant rather than lengthy education, and demanding but encouraging parents. The entrepreneur seeks high levels of achievement, is motivated to own and operate a business, has undertaken lots of planning, is happily married, is physically fit, tends toward aggressive (motivated by self-interest) and detached (independent and unemotional) modes of interpersonal behavior, and has the mental and emotional capacity to handle the task.

Allowing for the inevitable oversimplification of such a model, you can readily recognize many aspects of this stereotype. Most entrepreneurs enjoy talking about their childhoods, and most of the time their recollections of their earlier years make fascinating listening. They were interesting and unusual children carrying out duties around the house or delivering newspapers to earn money, or starting up collections of stamps, coins, rocks, and so on. Underlying these activities, which were ostensibly a source of fun, was always the prospect of gain and growth.

The mature entrepreneur's obsessive need to achieve may often be traced to his or her childhood relationship with the more dominant parent. Even if Mom or Dad was not a great commercial success, admiration and a desire for approval drove the child to prove himself or herself. Subtle signs of recognition from the parent, such as a nod or a smile, were cherished rewards. A surprisingly large number of entrepreneurs are the offspring of self-employed parents whose free spirit and independence rubbed off. In cases where the parent/child relationship was less cordial, even strained, the grown-up child may be out to "get even" by achieving a greater level of success in order to prove superiority. Finally, if there was no breadwinner because of death, divorce, or desertion during the entrepreneur's childhood, the child may have been forced to assume this role in the family. Inheriting a great deal of responsibility at an early age can speed along maturity, and with it enterprising tendencies.

What Are Your Motives and Qualifications?

The fact that you are reading this book probably means you consider yourself the enterprising type, and you may even have decided that you were, indeed, born to do business. But what is your motive for going out on your own?

Is it that you are just a dreamer? Are you sick and tired of being told what to do and you want your so-called freedom? Is it that you feel unappreciated or undervalued, or that you want to get back at the boss? Rather than good reasons to start your own business, these are simply reasons to quit your current job.

Is it that you want to make money? This must be one of your aims, but this motive alone is not enough to get you through the difficult years.

Don't go into business if you think that the grass is greener on the other side of the fence. Don't go into business if you have the attitude of a nine-to-fiver and enjoy such perks as company cars, luncheons, travel, and free pens. Along with these you will also have to say goodbye to your large pension or retirement and face up to the fact that the laws tend to be in the employee's favor, not the employer's. Don't go into business just because your friends do, because your family always has, or because you can't get permanent employment.

> **Case Study.** Sammy was only twenty-five. He had been married two or three years and had a very supportive wife. His older brother had a furniture business in which Sammy worked for wages. The brother constantly harassed Sammy and put him down. Sammy dreamed of going into business

for himself, but his motive was purely to beat his bullying brother, to avenge himself.

Well, he did. But he didn't do a business plan, and he didn't do anything else recommended in this book. The result was that within three months he hadn't sold any furniture, he couldn't pay his rent, and he had lost $15,000— his life savings.

Fortunately, he was young enough to recover his losses. And he also learned a lesson about healthy motives.

Starting a new business is not a time for self-deception. It is more often cause for great worry and tension as you put in long hours to do the necessary groundwork. Many small business operators risk not only their houses (to raise capital) but also their family life, their health, and their mental well-being. Big companies can afford to make some mistakes; small ones can't.

It is important to have positive reasons for going into business. Some sound motives, especially in combination, are to

- Develop a new sense of independence and freedom.
- Develop creative ideas.
- Achieve a better lifestyle.
- Build up a personal or family asset.
- Produce a particular product or service.
- Do things better than your employer does.

Equally important is to have the necessary practical qualifications. Are you self-disciplined, motivated, and creative? Are you versatile? Are you trained and experienced? Do you have knowledge of the industry you plan to go into? Do you have experience in it? Do you have the ability to motivate others? Do you have the willingness to learn? Do you have the support of your family? Do you have sufficient capital to finance the business? Do you have a strong work ethic? Do you have the ability to work under pressure?

Preparation for going into business involves a critical examination of your own characteristics and capabilities. Any shortcomings should be honestly admitted and sorted out by training or guidance.

Doing Your Homework

You do not have to go in blind. You can get help (and some relief from uncertainty) from courses, books, pamphlets, the government (U.S. Small Business Administration [SBA], Internal Revenue Service [IRS], etc.), professionals (accountants, lawyers, and so on), consultants, and the experience of others. That doesn't mean you have to take every course, read everything, and listen to everybody. What it does mean is that you should try to map out the terrain in which you intend to travel. Recognizing the importance of planning will set you apart from the majority of people in paid employment and those who fail in self-employment. Simply to survive in today's business environment (let alone to prosper), small business people must be better informed and more professional than ever before. They must grapple with a vast array of complex issues.

Before going into business, you should inform yourself about the general economy, government regulations, zoning regulations (state, federal, and local), and product standard regulations. Add to your list industrial relations, arbitration and conciliation, interest rates, exchange rates, levels of protection, levels of government and consumer spending, levels of taxation and grants, and export incentives and rebates.

Look at business in general: watch, learn, listen. Do your research, go to libraries, use all available government resources, attend employer associations, visit the Small Business Administration. There is a huge array of books available on small business, not just on how to do business plans but on specific subjects—various industries, franchising, and so on. Read the newspapers and business magazines, watch the Sunday morning business programs on television, and listen to the business shows on the radio. This way you will learn about the macroeconomic environment—in other words, what is happening with oil prices, real estate prices, the world economy, the national debt, the world peace program, and conservation issues. All the information that you gather from the media will eventually affect the way you run your business.

At first you may not realize how much you are learning and how it might relate to your circumstances, but eventually your knowledge will pay dividends and the relevance will become clear. If you understand what is happening in the world, you will be in a position to predict and respond to changes in interest rates, to make investment decisions, and to make sales.

Finally, you should undertake thorough research into the particular industry you are contemplating entering: its sales and profit trends, the effect of public opinion on profits, the level of imports, tariff protection, the economic cycles, characteristics of successful competitors, significant barriers to entry, spread of products, spread of customers, present market shares, and the standards for prices and products or promotions.

You should understand the requirements of your business and why a plan is so important (see Chapter 3), what cash reserves you need to contribute, what you need to borrow, what levels of skills and expertise you need, and what human resources you need to employ. You should assess the market and consumer needs as well as the effect of financial, legal, and personal aspects of your business plan, such as the need to get a long lease to protect your tenancy. You should assess the overhead involved: wages, electricity, rent, and so on.

If you are looking at buying an existing business (see Chapter 2), find out whether goodwill has been fairly assessed. Get sound accounting and legal advice appropriate to the business. Find out the lease conditions, patents, trade names, business names, sources of finance, financial management systems, bookkeeping procedures, stock-buying policies, and so on. It is a good idea to insist on a two-week trial period as a condition of sale to verify claims about turnover, gross and net profit, and average weekly net figures. Sit outside the business for a few days in a row. Witness the clientele first-hand; don't just rely on an accountant's figures (which might be rubbery).

In planning any business venture, begin by testing the water. Perhaps run a pilot before you commit yourself—work for someone in a similar industry, or work for the business you are thinking of buying. This enables you not only to learn about how that world operates, but also to pick up valuable ideas and perhaps even clients. The hidden agenda—the culture, the clients, the suppliers—contains valuable information. But make sure you do the work yourself; don't rely on anyone else. Whatever the product or service—scrap metal, hairdressing, engineering, graphic design—do your own research. Do your own homework.

Then do a careful analysis of your costs and returns. Make a realistic assessment of the competition and an honest appraisal of your own talents. Make sure you set up adequate and efficient management systems: They contribute more to business prosperity than marketing or production skills do. Make sure that you have clear objectives and be prepared to communicate these to all the people working for you and around you.

Be careful, but don't be intimidated by the things that could go wrong. Be aware when you are starting up that your competition could try to sabotage you. If you are determined and committed, you will see these obstacles through and you will prosper.

What if you do all your research, you do your pilot study, you begin your business plan, and then you decide not to go into business after all? You may decide that you are not really cut out for it now (not to say that you won't be in the future). Fine. You are better off turning back than pressing on. Continue to look at alternatives. Continue to do your research, especially into the market, to find the product or service that is going to be profitable. Look at different angles and marketing edges for ideas. Keep thinking, keep dreaming, keep looking, keep going to courses. Somewhere down the line you might be better situated to start an enterprise.

Developing Enterprising Habits

Providing you do decide to go ahead, make sure that you remain 100 percent committed to your decision: Believe in yourself and your ideas. Expect to succeed, and visualize that success by concentrating on developing certain key enterprising characteristics. These should include:

- Self-discipline (the ability to establish plans and rigidly adhere to them).
- Pleasing manner, honesty, trustworthiness, and reliability.
- Strong will to grow.
- Freedom in decision making and ideas.

- Interest in achievement.
- Little or no concern with status and the opinions of others.
- Farsightedness.
- Interpersonal skills to deal with people.
- Ability to exercise, and desire to retain, control.
- Delegation skills.
- Risk taking.
- Awareness of the need for profit and cash flow.
- Adaptability.
- Willingness to work long hours.
- Ability to find and defer to a mentor.

There is a slogan, "Work smarter, not harder." In hard times this should be modified to, "Work smarter, work harder, and work longer." But work only six days (as in the Bible), not seven. If you don't recharge your batteries, you will burn them out. Spend your day of leisure doing something you enjoy. Remember to balance the books of your personal life just as you balance your accounting books. It is important to keep things in perspective and realize that, as a human being, you have many parts to your life—your personal, spiritual, social, physical, and your work life—and all these parts function best when they are in harmony with each other.

Consider the cartoon of a man beneath which the caption read: "He spent his health to get his wealth and now he is spending his wealth to get his health again." Don't let it happen to you.

Develop trusting relationships with your business contacts—your bank manager, accountant, lawyer, customers, and suppliers. When your accountant gets twenty-five phone messages after having been out of the office for an hour, make sure he or she returns your call first because you are a friend; the same goes for your bank manager and your lawyer.

Identify with your business and enjoy it. After all, it is an expression of yourself, just like a painting, a poem, or a construction by a builder or an engineer. Remember, when you go into business you put yourself up there in lights, subjecting yourself to the scrutiny and criticism of the public, the government, unions, banks, and a host of other institutions, not to mention insecure individuals around you, especially those nonachievers who want to pull you down and make you pay for breaking away from the pack.

Don't let other people's attitudes get you down. Be patient and be understanding. Understand why people think the way they do and why they say what they do, especially your beloved partner or spouse. ("Where's your share of the bills?" "Why are you never home?" "Why don't you talk to me any more?" "We are drifting apart." "The kids need a father/mother.")

Recognize your own strengths and weaknesses, and learn to harness the former and compensate for the latter. Initially, when you start up your own business, you have to manage on whatever advice you can get from the outside. As time goes on you should be able to employ or pay for consultants to help you, or take on partners to make up for your weaknesses and give you added value, allowing you to spend most of your time doing the things you do best. If you are not sure what your weaknesses are, ask people who don't like you—they will soon tell you. Then go and ask people who like you. It may be that you have too many weaknesses to go into business. It is better to find this out in the planning process.

If you are facing problems, be strong. Don't let anyone else know. When you have cash flow problems the worst thing you can do is let your customers know it. Keep to yourself. Even in tough times, always have a bright, positive attitude toward life and people. Don't *ever* complain about your business. Never criticize your customers or your competition. If you do, you are putting yourself down.

Don't waste time and energy worrying about money problems. Try to look objectively at the problems, address the issues, and discover what is causing them. Is it lack of sales, lack of sales at the right price, lack of quality service, inability to collect money from customers, high overhead, high interest costs? Work out what the problem is and solve it. Use that energy positively, not negatively.

On the personal front, concentrate on maintaining stable relationships with your loved ones. Business is not good if it destroys relationships, as often happens, and it is very difficult to cope with the rigors and demands of a small business without a solid foundation at home. If you have a partner, you both need to be aware of the demands and stresses that a small business causes, not just in terms of cash flow but in the form of anxiety and other mental hardship, not to mention the spoiled dinners, forgotten birthdays, broken dates, and the insecurity of it all. Involve your partner in the business, not necessarily in the day-to-day affairs but in its commitment to success. This can only be done through concentrated communication—not necessarily every day, but perhaps once a week for an hour or so. Talk to each other so that you understand each other.

Learn to manage yourself, because if you can't, you certainly won't be able to manage a business. Time management is critical if you want to do justice to all aspects of your life. However, your loved ones need not only your time, but your energy as well. If you have children, it is a good idea to involve them in the business—let them come to the factory or the office. Of course they will say they don't want to and will get bored, but they have very attentive little ears that don't miss anything. This way they will learn about business well before you ever did. Let them see the good and bad sides of being self-employed. Should you have to work late one night, go to work late the next day or come home early. Go to the school, or go and watch your child play a sport in the middle of the afternoon. Do the unusual; be part of their life. Manage your time so you can spend quality time with your family. After all, remember why you are striving. Apart from the challenge of the process, it is to provide a better lifestyle for yourself and your family in the future.

Find time to have interests outside the business—recreational, social, and cultural. Leisure activity does more than rest your executive brain cells and make you a more balanced person. It gives you an interest that can continue into your retirement. Too many people devote their lives exclusively to work and are at a loss when they "retire." They are left with nothing to occupy their time or attention and often die of sheer boredom. No one is indispensable, as you will soon prove if your prolonged absence is forced through a nervous breakdown. So always take the vacation that you deserve. Apart from anything else, it is a good chance to see how well you have trained your second in command.

In a small business you need a huge amount of self-control, particularly in hard times. This is an important ingredient of executive efficiency. It enables you to adapt to changing conditions, to deal with emergencies, and to meet unexpected challenges calmly. People who regularly indulge in moods or fits of bad temper undermine their own authority and cease to command respect from those who work for them. They lose their sense of proportion and regard the smallest setback as a crisis. They antagonize and lose the cooperation of their subordinates. A few angry words can destroy in seconds the goodwill that has perhaps taken years to build up. But well-adjusted people who exercise self-discipline earn the respect of others and are at peace with themselves. They can carry responsibility without strain and keep calm in emergencies; in fact, they are sound and dependable always.

Self-employed people should have high standards. You should not ask others to do what you are not prepared to do yourself. You must be prepared to commit time and energy and to make some personal sacrifices. You must be completely loyal to the business and to your subordinates.

Throughout your business undertakings, never lose sight of the fact that the person behind the business matters more than the business in front of the person. So by all means enjoy what you do, but keep it in perspective and take care of yourself.

2

SETTING UP

To Establish or to Buy?

S hould you start a new business or buy one? It's a big decision, one that should normally be made during the development of the business plan (see Chapter 3).

Starting a New Business

Advantages

- You will have freedom of choice in all aspects of the business.
- If you have limited capital, you can start on a small scale without having to pay for goodwill.
- You can break new ground with a new idea.

Disadvantages

- It takes more time, effort, and hard work to start up a new business.
- Time must be spent working up a clientele, developing lines of credit and supply, and building up experienced staff.
- The future is uncertain.

Buying an Existing Business

Advantages

- Sales to existing customers provide instant income and a known cash flow.
- Relationships with banks, suppliers, and so on are already established.
- You can work with a vendor before and after the sale to get advice and perhaps help with some secondary financing.

Disadvantages

- Image and policies can be difficult to change.
- The business may have depended heavily on the people you are buying it from—on their terms, personality, and contacts—and may suffer from their departure.
- It is difficult to establish the value of the business. Be aware that the person selling the business will probably want more than it is really worth.

Ultimately, the decision whether to buy or start a new business has a lot to do with what makes you feel comfortable. If you don't have years of experience in the relevant area, it may be safer to buy someone else's experience, rather than try to learn from scratch and make lots of mistakes.

However, providing you follow the advice already offered in this book—do your research, run a pilot, work for somebody else—my advice is to start up your own business. Although both options carry dangers and risks, in my opinion it is safer to start with a clean slate. Otherwise, you don't know what sort of problems you might be buying.

In hard times, although there are so many cheap businesses around, there is also a proliferation of contingent liabilities. You could walk in and take over a printing business, for example, and all of a sudden find that the finance company comes to repossess the press. It is what you don't know that might harm you most. You don't know whether facts and figures have been falsified, or whether economic circumstances might change the positive projections. A new zoning ordinance might be about to come through that will affect the location of your business, or a new competitive product might be about to swamp yours or undercut it in price. Even if the existing owners know about these things, they might hesitate to disclose such negative information.

If, despite the dangers, you decide to buy, a number of key issues should be carefully considered. First, if the business is so profitable, why is the existing owner selling? Don't accept his or her word. Make your own discreet inquiries to establish the reason. Park outside the building or the office and carry out a thorough survey of the business. If it is a retail business, observe it at different times and on different days to assess the number of customers. Don't accept figures prepared by others—even from the owner's accountant. Do your own research.

How long has the business been on the market? A seasonal business should be bought only with careful timing. All other things being equal, it would be unwise, for instance, to miss a Christmas boom or go into an ice-cream business in autumn, especially if there are no cash reserves for the business to fall back on.

If the business is a limited company and you are acquiring the shares, seek legal advice about the liabilities you are assuming. The vendor's indemnities may be useless if they are not supported by assets. Check to see whether you will be eligible or liable for any current debts or credits or for any other payments due.

Goodwill is difficult to define, but basically it is the hope, and no more, that existing customers will continue to support the business under new ownership. You will probably have to pay for this asset, which depends heavily on past profits, locality, competition in the area, and the previous owner's personality. Your accountant and banker should be able to guide you on this point.

If the business will be relying on local trade, make sure you know the area well. Walk around and get a feeling for the neighborhood. Is it declining or growing? What developments are taking place or being planned? Visit local authorities and other businesses to get answers to these questions.

At a minimum it is essential to obtain the last three years' audited financial statements to provide some indication of turnover and profit. Go through the figures with your accountant and banker and adjust them if necessary.

Talk to the suppliers and see whether they will stay with you. Look carefully at all the overhead and costs. Try to determine what costs will change if you take over, whether they will increase or decrease, and whether there will be different kinds of costs.

Make sure your lease is long enough, not only for you to stay there but for you to fulfill whatever your business plan suggests. If you plan to sell the concern, make sure your lease has five or six years still to run.

If staff are employed, how well trained or qualified are they? Will they stay on? Specialized personnel in particular should be retained if possible.

To summarize, your evaluation of whether to buy the business should include

- Evaluation of why the current owner is selling. (Is it due to ill health or retirement, or is there something he or she knows that you don't—planned highway construction or some other reason for expected loss of business?)
- Assessment of what you are buying and how much you are spending, whether you are borrowing or using your own capital, and whether you are going to get a return on that. If you are borrowing money, determine whether you are going to get enough profit to cover all costs, including interest on the loan.
- Examination of a detailed breakdown of all sales, expenses, and profit, both past and projected. This needs to be audited and checked independently. It won't contain warning bells because, unfortunately, there are not many totally honest vendors.

Buying a business without checking these things is like buying a house without inspecting it thoroughly. Free advice on the process can be obtained from a number of sources: the bank, trade associations, employer groups, neighboring businesses, suppliers to the business, or even local truck drivers. They can all be indirect sources of information about whether you should buy the business.

The next thing you should do is look at the assets. Do this in detail. Stock should be readily saleable and not stale (if perishable) or obsolete. Equipment needs to be reasonably modern and in working order. Replacement costs may put a burden on the business sooner than expected. Calculate conservatively what the stock is worth, whether the price is accurate, what competition it has, as well as its quality, style, condition, balance, and suitability. Is there too much stock or not enough stock being carried? Also, what furniture, fittings, and equipment are included in the sale? How old are they; do they need to be replaced; are they in good repair; will they fall apart; what maintenance agreements are on them? Also, how collectible are the debts and who will collect them (are they part of the purchase)?

Get customer lists, business and client records, and any other assets that are available, such as trademarks. Are there many customers with a personal attachment to the seller? If you are going to lose customers because of this, the purchase price should be reduced accordingly.

You should also look at the liabilities, both obvious and contingent. This area takes a lot of work. What monies are owing to creditors; when are they payable and who is responsible for paying them? Which taxes haven't been paid? What liens are there? What mortgages exist against the assets of the business? Just to get a letter of indemnity from the vendor isn't good enough, particularly if there is any doubt as to his or her financial strength. Don't rely on the vendor's statement. It often overstates turnover, sales income, and expenses. Beware of any financial statements that are not signed by an accountant. (Accountants can be sued for signing off on any information that is incorrect.)

Whenever you buy a business, engage the services of a lawyer as well as an accountant to make sure nothing is missed, that all the i's are dotted and the t's crossed. Make sure your purchase will actually give you a return on your investment and help you achieve the objectives in your business plan. Have an agreement written into the contract of sale that you will be permitted to work in the business with the current proprietor for four weeks prior to settlement, and that he or she agrees to continue working with you for a changeover period of four weeks after settlement. This should alert you to any possible misrepresentations or problems, and ensure a smooth transition of ownership.

It is important to cover, and get in writing, a number of essential points, including a list of all the assets and liabilities purchased and a statement that actual ownership does transfer in terms of title details, vehicle registration, and so forth. It must be clearly set out who is taking responsibility for what liabilities.

If the business you are buying is a partnership, you should get a copy of the partnership agreement. If there is no written agreement, you should find out who the partners are and whether they have authority to sell the business with its assets. It may be advisable to obtain an agreement from the seller to ensure that he or she will not compete with the buyer in the same line of business for a specified period of time within a certain radius of the buyer.

If the business you are buying is a company, you should get a certified copy of the resolution of the shareholders' meeting on the sale of the assets. In addition, you should obtain copies of the bylaws and articles of incorporation, share transfer books, and minutes of shareholders' and directors' meetings. Consider deferring payment to the seller in the event of misrepresentation, default in the seller's promise not to compete, or default in a contingent liability.

The most difficult factor in buying a business is arriving at the price, with the value of goodwill usually being the stumbling block. This book's purpose is not to discuss how to calculate selling or buying prices. Most general references on small business cover this topic specifically.

Franchises

A business opportunity that is growing in popularity is the franchise. The essence of franchising is that one party, the franchiser—who has a product, process, trade name, service, or system—enters into an agreement with another party, the franchisee, whereby the franchisee is authorized to sell the product or the process. (Such agreements are also known as dealership licenses and distributorships.) The franchiser, in return, is paid by the franchisee. The size and the form of the payment can vary according to the type of business and whether the franchiser is new or well established. The franchiser will normally look after advertising and training and will provide merchandise and advice.

Because of these support systems, many small businesses start by buying a franchise. Although such arrangements rarely generate a fortune, your money can buy you good experience. However, caution should be exercised. There are some major traps in buying a franchise, not the least of which is the financial strength of the franchiser. Before taking on such a partner, (and this is how you must see the franchiser, as your business partner), obtain bank references for the franchise.

Advantages

- It gives the small business operator an opportunity to participate in a much larger business, enabling his or her capital contribution to go further and lowering the cost of entering at that level of business.
- The business is usually supported by marketing arrangements.
- If management systems and training are in place and enhance efficiency, the risk of failure is theoretically reduced.
- Profitability in a franchise business is, theoretically, generally higher. This allows the franchiser to expand the business more quickly at a lower capital

cost and provides for better control. Because of the financial commitment and personal qualities of the franchisee as business owner and employee, he or she is more likely to contribute toward higher profit.

Disadvantages

- There is a risk that the franchiser might collapse as the result of inexperience or financial instability.
- The well-conducted franchise will be closely controlled. Hence, the franchisee will lose some independence, and this may cause disillusionment.
- The business may turn out to be a fad.
- The franchise arrangement might be a vehicle for fraud.
- The franchiser might have drawn up the agreement to ensure that it protects his or her interests only.

The purchase of a franchise should be contemplated in exactly the same way as any small business purchase and with just as much care.

Small Business Structures

If you elect to set up your own business, one of the earliest decisions you will face is how to structure it. Four options are available, and careful thought should be given to each one. Your accountant should assist you in making your choice, which should be governed by the nature of the business, its estimated profitability, and the degree of financial risk.

1. Sole Proprietorships

If you want to run a business by yourself, the simplest and cheapest structure to adopt is that of sole proprietor or sole operator. This can be done with the minimum of legal formalities and requirements. An individual may wish to operate under his or her own name, but any other business name that has not previously been used may be selected and registered in your state.

Advantages

- A sole proprietor benefits directly from all profits and holds and owns legal title to all the business assets (tangible and intangible), to equipment, and to any goodwill. Any losses incurred by the business can be used to reduce income from other sources.
- It is easy to start up and shut down, and reporting requirements and government regulations are simpler than for other forms of business.

Disadvantages

- Management expertise may be limited, being restricted to the competence and skill of the individual owner unless there are other salaried staff.
- Additional capital may be limited by its dependence on the personal credit rating of the sole proprietor.
- The owner has unlimited personal liability.
- The business is viable only while the owner does not suffer accident, disability, or death. Insurance must be taken out to provide for these risks.
- All business profits are taxed at personal rates, which may be higher than other marginal tax rates.
- Taxes are payable by the self-employed person on a quarterly basis, which can be crippling in the early stages of the business.

- The owner is often forced to make all the decisions without the opportunity to test the ideas of others.
- In the eyes of the law, you and the business are one. If things go wrong you cannot blame anyone else in the business. If bankruptcy occurs, all your assets will go into a pool to pay creditors.

The continued prosperity of a sole proprietorship depends to an enormous extent upon the continuing credit, discipline, skill, knowledge, ability, judgment, experience, personality, relationships, and quality of life of the sole proprietor.

To summarize, the major advantage of a sole proprietorship is the ease of setup and administration. Despite the major disadvantage of unlimited liability, my advice to people starting a new business is to do so as a sole operator and to review their situations regularly.

2. Partnerships

The next most common form of business structure is the partnership, including those formed by husbands and wives for tax purposes. A business partnership is simply a relationship that exists between two or more people or entities who come together in order to carry on an enterprise with a view to making a profit.

If you are considering this type of business structure, ask yourself why you want to take on a partner. Don't do it for the wrong reasons—for example, financial advantage or because you need a vacation. A business partner should contribute value to the business other than just money; he or she should contribute skills that are additional or complementary to yours. Partnerships, like marriages, can be fantastic if they work out, but if they fail—if one partner becomes a liability rather than an asset—they can become real problems and cause severe financial damage.

When the strengths and weaknesses of each partner are well balanced, the business will benefit. If the balance is uneven, the partnership itself may become the business's worst enemy. It is probably no accident that some of the greatest enterprising successes have been solo acts.

One of the most common reasons for the failure of both marriages and businesses is that people don't communicate with each other. They don't meet; they are not honest with each other; they don't face the real issues and the problems. That is why all business partners should be prepared to have lots of meetings, most of them formalized, and to make a real effort to communicate.

Advantages

- The administrative procedures associated with establishing a new business partnership are relatively simple and inexpensive. Once a business name has been registered, the operation is simple to understand and run.

- This type of structure enhances the respective partners' complementary skills and allows their strengths and weaknesses to offset each other. It also enables individuals to achieve more than they might on their own, the whole often being greater than the sum of its parts.

- There is little legal interference from government bodies.

- It is more likely that additional capital can be raised where there is more than one person involved.

- The business is less vulnerable to any one individual's disability through sickness, accident, or death.

Disadvantages

- Each partner still has unlimited personal liability and is responsible for the activities of the other partner(s). Unlimited personal liability attaches to the partners for any and all debts of the partnership. This can jeopardize the personal estate of either partner.
- Partners are mutually bound, obligated, and personally responsible for one another's professional actions.
- It is difficult to change partners, particularly when disputes arise. This can cause a great deal of personal anxiety and even financial loss.
- Where the partners' contributions each have a negative (rather than a positive) value, the principle that the whole can be greater than the sum of its parts works devastatingly in reverse. It is difficult to calculate the values of respective contributions for the purposes of dissolving the partnership.

All partnerships should have agreements. An oral agreement will not do. An agreement should *always* be in writing. In fact, for best results, a lawyer who is independent of both parties should be used to draw it up. All aspects of the operation and control of the business should be agreed on and should be covered in the partnership agreement. Make sure, in particular, that it contains very clear exit clauses so that each partner is aware of his or her precise obligations on breakup. In the absence of a written agreement, all partners, whether there are two with 50 percent each or three with 33⅓ percent, will always be considered equal. When all is said and done, a partnership is risky, but if properly run, with communication and thorough documentation, a partnership can be a highly productive option.

One way to avoid conflict in a partnership is to make the trading activity your only joint investment activity and, indeed, social activity. If you are going to buy other properties or other businesses, or borrow money, do it separately from your partner. Go to different banks and buy your other investments in your own name or in the family name. The problems associated with having all your businesses with the same bank can be horrific if you need to dissolve the partnership. The cost, particularly if there is conflict, can undo any profit that might have been achieved.

It comes back to one of the principles of life in general: If something is going well in one situation or with one person, don't try to duplicate it elsewhere. Don't get too familiar with your partner(s). Keep out of each other's pockets. Don't go to the same social functions. Don't go on vacations together. Don't even have the same hobbies. Above all, don't have the same accountant. An accountant cannot be independent when acting for more than one party in a partnership. He or she is likely to be biased toward the partner who brought in the new business. For this reason, it is critical to have separate accountants for each of the partners and one for the entity itself.

A business partner should be chosen with great care. In many ways the requirements are like those for choosing a spouse. (Remember, more waking hours are spent at work than at home.) Therefore, try to imagine living with your prospective partner for the rest of your life.

By the same token, your best friend is not necessarily the ideal person to go into business with, because you are probably too much alike. Your strengths and weaknesses are likely to be the same, which is counterproductive in business. Consider, for example, two people who are good friends, who play a sport, and go out socially together. They decide to form a business partnership, but they are both salespeople. Unless they employ other people, how can they possibly offset their weaknesses against one another? Although they get along well socially, in business they will probably clash and not give each other added value. If you intend to go into business with another person, you should get someone who is good at whatever you are poor at. If you are a salesperson, for example, get someone who is good at finance and accounting or production. Get someone who is good at selling if you are not.

Many successful partnerships have been formed by people who grew up together and went into business when they were age twenty or so. In such cases, even though there tends to be one dominant personality, they can work together. If they are still working well together by the time they are thirty, their partnership tends to last forever.

Husband/wife partnerships can work, but only if they are very well planned and clear lines are drawn between business and personal issues. Set aside certain times of the day at home when you don't discuss anything to do with the business. This is particularly important when the business has cash flow pressures. Hard times commonly take their toll on marriage/business partnerships.

One of the biggest problems with partnerships is that people keep changing all the time. Personalities change with age, and individual circumstances change, for example through divorce or the death of a loved one. A number of factors can influence the personal basis of the partnership, and this source of potential problems needs to be closely monitored and worked on.

One of the ways to ensure that a partnership works is to take a vacation together at least once every twelve months to communicate—thrash out problems, plan the next year, work on your business plan. It need not necessarily be an expensive vacation. Go for a weekend to a country resort where it is quiet and relaxing, where you are away from the day-to-day hassles of the business and the demands of your family—a place where you can sort out any personality problems in peace and privacy with a bit of relaxation thrown in. One partnership I know meets once a week for dinner. Eight years on, the two partners are still together, still growing, and still successful.

> **Case Study.** George went into partnership in a small driver training business. Overhead was fairly low, but they were running five or six leased cars. They had opted for long terms with high residual payouts in order to minimize their leasing costs.
>
> Business was going well until George's wife demanded that he spend more time with her, bring home more money for more trips, let her use one of the business cars, and so on. George's partner, Paul, also started to spend less time in the business, to draw out more money, and to use the cars for private purposes. The business developed cash flow problems.
>
> One day a bitter quarrel broke out between George and Paul. But there was no documentation to cover their respective legal rights; they didn't even have a partnership agreement. Initially, George stayed away and let Paul run the business on his own. Six months later they bumped into each other. Paul said, "I think I know what's wrong now. I have been taking too much money out of the business and I haven't been working hard enough. The $10,000 overdraft is now $50,000, I am three months behind with lease payments on all the cars, and the finance company is threatening to repossess them." Paul was physically ill and appealed to George for help.
>
> George really had no moral obligation, but he certainly had a financial one. He had two options: to walk away with a debt of $50,000 plus leases—approximately $250,000 worth of liability exposure—or to go back into the business.

He went back into the business. He had a meeting with the bank, prepared a business plan with the help of a credible accountant, and asked the creditors for a twelve-month moratorium. Everyone gave George a chance. He worked very hard for the next year and spent little time at home, despite his family problems. He got his overdraft back below $10,000 and refinanced his cars with low residuals and short payout periods. He was back on top. But whether George or Paul will ever go into partnership again is another matter.

3. Companies

In legal terms, the company is the most complex business structure normally available to small business. Basically, it separates the assets and liabilities of the business from those of the individual proprietor. The company, therefore, becomes a legal entity in its own right. This means it can sue or be sued independently of its officers and directors. More importantly, its members (that is, its shareholders) are limited in their personal liability. If the company goes into liquidation and there are no personal guarantees or other forms of security offered, the shareholders are liable only to the extent of any unpaid capital.

The laws and requirements for running companies are increasing and becoming more complex, primarily with the intention of protecting the rights of investors. The company structure should be considered only once the business has been operating for a while and has shown an ability to earn consistent profits. It will protect the owner's personal assets unless personal guarantees or securities are given to banks or creditors.

Advantages

- A key advantage is that of limited liability. Investors in a corporation avoid the total exposure of sole proprietorships or partnerships.
- Companies can pay dividends.
- The company has continued life and can be bought and sold. It is easy to transfer ownership.
- A company's board of experienced and knowledgeable members can provide sound advice and counsel.
- Directors can raise capital by the introduction of additional owners (and therefore additional investors), which will, of course, be easier if the business prospers in the first place.

Disadvantages

- This structure is comparatively expensive to set up and maintain.
- This structure is becoming heavily regulated and costly to operate.
- It is complex to operate and especially to dissolve.
- Shareholders do not have complete management control but do have a say in the appointment of directors.
- Directors are legally responsible not only to the shareholders or the owners of the business who appoint them, but also to the regulatory agencies, their customers, and their creditors or anyone from whom they borrow money. They are subject to numerous government statutory requirements, and the onus is on them to ensure the company is trading profitably.

4. Trusts

A variation of the company structure, and one that is a bit more flexible, is the trust. A trust is simply a vehicle for someone to pledge to look after someone else's money, not unlike a will. The beneficiaries of a trust are like the beneficiaries of a decedent's estate. A trust is even more complex to operate and establish than a company and requires that the entrepreneur understand his or her obligations under trust law as well as company law. Even if a trust is deemed to be the best vehicle eventually, it should not be adopted until the business's profit potential is fully realized.

A trustee holds the trust property and runs the trust business on behalf of the beneficiary specified in the trust deed. A trust has no right to act on its own because it is not a legal entity. It can act only via a trustee, which can be a natural person or even a company. It is more common for companies, rather than individuals, to be appointed as trustees.

All options for business structures should be examined, but remember that when you are first starting off, it is better to keep things simple and keep costs down. If it appears that consistent high profits and significant taxes are going to occur, then more sophisticated and more complicated structures, such as companies and trusts, should be considered. However, you are not expected to know all the ins and outs of business structures, particularly from the point of view of tax planning; that is the role of your carefully selected accountant.

Protecting Your Hard-Earned Wealth

The appropriate time to protect your wealth is before you have even accumulated it. It is too late to start doing anything about it when your business is already in financial trouble.

The legal system set up to "collect" from failed companies is comprehensive and effective, and the courts commonly set aside any elaborate and costly schemes that entrepreneurs might devise in a last-ditch attempt to save their hard-earned personal assets in the midst of a business collapse. Rather, some simple measures to quarantine assets should be taken while you are setting up your business. Consult a competent lawyer on the details of these.

In the case of a marriage, the partner who runs the business should not be the partner in whose name the family assets are owned. The assets should be held in the name of the spouse or in the name of a separate trust or company. The person owning the assets should not become a director of the company, never sign a personal guarantee, and never allow his or her assets to be used as security. The owner of the assets must be able to demonstrate that he or she was able to purchase the assets using his or her own income and that the partner involved in the business did not contribute in any way to their purchase.

The sorts of structures that will serve to protect your personal wealth may not always be the most tax effective. But the long-term benefits to yourself and your family should take priority over tax considerations. These structures might also cause some problems in the event of divorce; however, few marriage partners would disagree that it is better to fight over getting less than half of a one-dollar surplus than to be one dollar in debt and have nothing to fight over!

Some Words of Caution

Anyone considering going into business should be aware of the existence of credit bureaus. These companies record borrowing and payment histories and are available to lenders and certain other entities. They record who has checked you before and whether there have been any defaults or court judgments against you.

Your credit report is of supreme importance. If it contains a negative note, you will not be able to borrow money and you will have trouble attracting investors. Any default or judgment entry against you may stay in place for years. The only way to eliminate it is to contact the entity that put it there and ask them to remove it.

If your report contains any negative information, be honest about it when you are seeking financing or investment. Prepare a written explanation of the circumstances of your default and how it was resolved. Get lawyers' and accountants' letters of support as well. Don't try to borrow money hoping that no one will notice your report—especially in difficult times, which call for greater caution on the part of the lender. If everyone was honest in the first place there wouldn't be the need for a credit report; in fact, there wouldn't be the need for mortgages. That is why it is so important to confront the situation with complete honesty.

> **Case Study.** Sarah had a small advertising business. She leased her computer hardware from a finance company linked to the supplier and arranged for her monthly payments to be debited directly to her bank account. When she changed branches and office address mid-term, the direct debit was not transferred by the bank and fell by the wayside. This went unnoticed by Sarah and her accountant until her accountant was contacted by the finance company, who assumed she had gone out of business. The matter was promptly and amicably rectified with a lump-sum back

payment. In the meantime, however, the finance company had filed a default against Sarah's company, but it was subsequently marked "paid." Sarah has since been successful in having the entry removed.

You must also familiarize yourself with the implications of personal guarantees. When you finance your car you sign a personal guarantee, which literally means that if you can't make a payment on the due date the finance company has the right to come and repossess the car and take the furniture out of your house. Almost everyone in business will be required to sign a personal guarantee sooner or later, especially in hard times. When you lease your premises, when you sign a rental agreement, when you obtain finance from the bank, you will be required to sign a personal guarantee. In most cases you have no alternative, but to retain control you must keep a register of what you have signed. When the various contracts are released, make sure the personal guarantees are released. Make sure you have the contract canceled and you get a letter to that effect from the financial institution. If one partner in a partnership is bought out, or you want to sell out yourself, make sure any finance documentation is completely rewritten. Don't rely on third-party letters or indemnities; they are not strong enough and don't give any protection at all.

Finally, a warning: The most common causes of small business failure are lack of planning, inexperience, and incompetence. These usually manifest themselves as

- Failure to seek advice, especially financial.
- Failure to keep adequate and accurate financial records.
- Inadequate market research at the outset.
- Deteriorating cash flow and working capital.
- Growing too big too fast.

- Poor location.
- Inadequate promotion and advertising.
- Poor knowledge of competition affecting price and marketing policies.
- Excessive personal draws for private use (motor vehicle, holidays).
- Failure to maintain cash reserves for contingencies.
- Overextension of credit, excessive overdraft, and loans, causing liquidity problems.
- High interest costs.
- Financing expansion with interest rates higher than can be earned by the funds borrowed.
- Lack of time management.
- Failure to insure against possible risks.
- Inability to assess a risk and act appropriately.
- Inability to motivate employees.
- Failure to see macroeconomic, social, and political trends, to understand how these might affect the business, and to be flexible enough to be able to benefit from them.

Be aware of these pitfalls, and guard against them by doing your research, being careful, keeping your eyes wide open, talking to lots of people, and learning as much as you can.

Case Study. Michael was a very enterprising person with a rural background. The only form of employment he knew was self-employment, but he knew nothing about running a business, small or large, or about borrowing, marketing, and finance. All he had was an enormous belief in his own ability. At twenty-four he set up his first legal business. With his innate marketing flair, his business grew rapidly. Clients came from all directions—even from other states and overseas. Things just kept going from good to better.

He never even thought about cash flow, didn't discuss plans, just went with the tide. The economy was booming. Not all his customers paid, but enough money came in to support his lifestyle and business ambitions.

Michael diversified into property investments, convention businesses, marketing businesses, and publishing businesses. Within three years he had a whole range of investments, none of which he monitored or followed through on. He had a terrible habit of setting up something, getting bored, and moving on, without paying any attention to detail. He didn't know what business he was in and he didn't really care; he just wanted to keep growing and feeding his ego, not his bank balance. Because he was able to make a good case and present some convincing figures, he was quite good at borrowing money.

One day the economy turned. Sales stopped coming in. Various partners and directors of the companies he had set up turned against him because conditions were tough. He had signed numerous guarantees for various rental properties, cars, and equipment. He had worked long hours and hadn't paid himself a cent. He had just lived off the businesses and hadn't put away any money. In fact, he had built up some private debt and didn't even realize he had done it. It had been so easy to borrow. Sure he diversified, but none of his investments returned any money.

Michael eventually came to realize that, despite his energy, work ethic, and earlier prosperity, things were going rapidly against him. He hadn't paid enough attention to cash flow and profit. There was more cash going out than coming in. He hadn't stayed on course and concentrated on his legal practice and legal expertise.

Three years down the road, having paid out something like $300,000 in personal guarantees and $200,000 in legal fees (not to mention the price of recriminations, innuendos, and threats), he now knows where he is at. He knows what business he's in, concentrates on cash flow, and prepares business plans every six months. He makes the hard decisions, knows his break-even point, knows exactly what his costs are per month, per week, per day, and has his ego in shape.

When first starting off, by all means have vision but don't have grand schemes. Be modest and careful. In the early stages, the fewer people involved the better, given your limited financial resources. The best time to take on staff or partners is when you are up and running. Do everything yourself at first, get your hands dirty, and understand how everything works in your business before employing someone else to do it for you. That way you fully understand what is involved and can keep a hand in it even though you may not be there on a daily basis. Don't think you can come in at the top; in your own business it is better to start at the bottom and work your way up. Starting on your own also keeps the overhead down. It's best to be cautious first, to tread very slowly and carefully.

Small businesses face many problems—how to talk to the bank manager, how to handle an irate creditor, whether to buy this way or that way, whether to purchase new equipment, whether to work longer hours, whether to go on that business trip. Here is a formula for all these decisions. First, the most important person in your life is you and by implication your family. So, whatever decision you make on any of these complex issues must be on the grounds of what is best for you and your family. Second, consider what is best for cash flow. That means profit, or what is left after the sale has been made. Third and last, consider what's best for tax purposes. Of course, taxes are important. If you have a tax problem, though, you should be pleased because it means you are making a profit. Make sure you keep your eye on taxes and don't just leave tax considerations until the end of the financial year. You must constantly monitor the taxation environment because it is always changing, but never let taxes become a preoccupation in your decision making.

3

THE BUSINESS PLAN

Every small business must be built on solid ground. Like a tall building, it needs a firm foundation to anchor it in strong winds. The basis of a firm foundation is planning. "To fail to plan is to plan to fail," as the saying goes.

The ideal approach to general planning is to go somewhere, away from all the struggles, constraints, and ambitions of your day-to-day life. Then free your mind and write down what you really want and how you are going to achieve it.

Ask yourself the following questions:

- How much money do I want to make?
- How many years do I want to work?
- What sort of home do I want?
- What sort of lifestyle do I want?
- What sort of restaurants do I want to go to?
- How many holidays do I want to have?
- What sort of things do I like doing?
- How many sports do I want to play?
- Do I want employees, and, if so, how many?
- What sort of customers do I want?
- What will all of this cost?

Write down the answers. Putting things on paper serves to crystallize your thinking. It takes things off your mind, freeing up space that could be used for something else—for remembering something you haven't done, for developing a new idea, or for solving a problem.

Once you have listed your thoughts, you can easily form them into a logical personal plan. If you don't plan and set goals, you are not likely to achieve anything. It is just like playing most competitive sports. Without goals and a strategy for scoring, what is the point of the game? The details (for example, how many hours you want to work) may change from year to year, but the overall aims will remain in place.

If you are serious about being successful in business and making money, a business plan is as fundamental to the life of your business as genes are to human biology. In its absence, Simon's Law will prevail: "Routine drives out planning; the urgent takes priority over the important." The longer the time taken to develop your business plan, the better it is likely to be. The more you have thought through what can go wrong and what you can do about fixing it, the slimmer the chance that mistakes will occur and the greater your ability to deal with those that do.

The business plan must recognize and be consistent with the external environment and take into account economic factors, opportunities, and risks. But it must also acknowledge the personal—your current resources, skills, strengths, and weaknesses. It is not something you can delegate; it must come from you. Don't say that you don't have the time, that you know what the problems are so you don't have to put them on paper, that the job changes from month to month and you cannot plan in advance, that you will wait until things happen and will act accordingly. These are avoidance tactics.

A goal without a plan is a dream. There is plenty of evidence to show that businesses that develop and use formal plans have a greater chance of surviving than those that do not, irrespective of their size, especially in difficult times. The question is not "Should I plan?" but rather "How should I go about it?"

The Ideal Plan

The perfect plan is one that helps you achieve your goals and objectives. It passes a "SWOT" analysis—it capitalizes on your Strengths and overcomes your Weaknesses while taking advantage of external Opportunities and, wherever possible, minimizing external Threats.

The ideal plan is one that you constantly refer to and review. It is continually changing and evolving, and constantly being updated, upgraded, and modified to account for changed circumstances. It benefits a number of parties—including staff, banks, and customers. At each appropriate stage you should submit the plan to your accountant and other chosen advisers who should prompt, guide, encourage, and redirect you in its development.

The business plan is your statement of how you are going to perform in your business. It sets out in detail all your goals and objectives, both personal and professional. It should include market research and analysis, and a feasibility study of your planned enterprise. It should also include a marketing plan showing projected sales volume (or number of products or hours of work).

The business plan tells you what production, administrative, and personnel facilities you will need to provide the level of turnover budgeted. It tells you what tools of trade are required and in what location. Then it tells you how such a venture will be financed—with how much, in what mix (your own funds and those of investors and lenders), and with what equity ratio between each. Clearly, the most important of these is raising financing. Going into business is costly, but finding capital to start up and finance growth is one of the toughest problems the entrepreneur faces, especially in times of tight lending policies and high interest rates. It is critical that the business plan identifies the exact capital requirements and the correct financing mix.

Once the plan is drawn up, it must be discussed among the business's owners, directors, advisers, and investors. Meetings are held to discuss it, suggestions are made, and the whole thing starts all over again. So, apart from being used by you personally, it should also be used by all those around you, including your senior executives. It is a template for the coordination of activity, designed to keep everyone on track and heading in the same direction.

Used outside your operation, the business plan is a vital sales tool. It shows lenders, investors, bankers, customers, and suppliers that you and your partners have enough skill and experience in your chosen business area to seek opportunities, manage effectively, solve problems, and make profits. As such, it should enable you to obtain the goods, credit, and financing you desire.

Your plan should cover all the major issues and yet not be so detailed that the reader is turned off. Common sense should prevail. The guidelines set out in this chapter cover a wide variety of manufacturing and servicing businesses and should not be followed slavishly. For example, a plan for a service business clearly does not require any discussion of manufacturing or product design.

Be realistic in your plan. Start small and keep it simple. Don't have overly ambitious goals. It is better to have lower goals at first so you can get a sense of achievement. Don't stretch yourself to the point where every last dollar is riding on everything going right. In your decision making, budgeting, and planning, always allow for things to go wrong. The plan shouldn't be rushed; it is not something that can be created in a busy day. It might best be achieved during a weekend away with your partners, mentors, or advisers (see Chapter 6). Then, you need to sleep on it.

The primary objective in writing a business plan is to shape it for the audience for which it is intended, taking into account that the potential investor/lender is likely initially to devote only five minutes to reading it.

The following pages set out a generic description of what should be included in your plan. It can be adapted to your individual situation, from a simple takeout food operation to a satellite technology business. The end result might be as long as fifty pages or as short as three.

Read this section two or three times before beginning your plan and refer to the relevant parts as you go. Answer the questions, be prompted by the information, respond to the suggestions, and complete your plan accordingly.

The Summary

A summary at the beginning is critical and should emphasize exactly what the potential investors or lenders want to know, without exaggeration or untruths. It should constitute about one-tenth of the whole and should give the reader an idea of whether it is worth his or her time to review the rest of the plan.

Write your summary only after you have written your plan. As you draft each section of the plan, highlight a few sentences that you think are important enough to be included in the summary. Allow plenty of time to write the summary. Remember that it is probably the first thing about you and your business that the would-be investor or lender is going to read. Unless it is appealing and convincing, it may also be the last!

Your summary should contain very brief statements about the following:

1. Your business's origins, activities, management, and performance.
2. Any distinguishing features of your product or service.
3. The market attraction.
4. Your financial projections.
5. The amount of money you are seeking, in what form (equity or borrowing or both), and for what purpose.

Try to persuade several people to review your summary in draft form. They should be people (such as your mentor) whose business acumen you respect but who are not involved in your venture. Then evaluate their reactions realistically. Did they quickly grasp what you are proposing to do? Were they "turned on" by what they read? Did they ask you whether they could invest? Their reactions should provide you with some useful indications of how the lender or investor is likely to react.

The summary is then followed by the plan itself, organized along the lines of the following headings.

The Introduction

By way of introduction, describe your business and the industry to which it belongs. In this section, you should provide the reader with some background on what you are going to present in subsequent sections about your product or service, your market opportunity, and the people and plans that you have for going after that opportunity. You should briefly describe to whom the product or service is being offered, and sketch the nature and current condition of your industry to show where and how you fit into it.

Your Business

Describe the business you are in or intend to enter. Describe your product or services, possible customers, and regions of operation. Trace the history of your business: when it was formed, how its products or services were chosen and developed, and what role each of the principals has played in bringing the business to where it is today.

If your business is already trading and is now seeking to expand, review its market penetration and its financial performance (sales, profits, return on equity). If, as is to be expected, your business has had early setbacks and incurred losses, describe these and say what you are doing to avoid recurrences. Your proposal might appear too good to be true if you omit all reference to past problems, and these can be readily determined from your credit report (see "Some Words of Caution," Chapter 2).

Your Industry

Present your view of the nature, current status, and prospects for the industry in which your business operates or will operate. Without going into too much detail, describe in two or three sentences each of the following: the principal participants and how they are performing; growth in sales and profits and any published forecasts for the current year; companies that have recently entered or left these markets and why; and what major economic, social, technological, or regulatory trends are affecting or are likely to affect your business.

Features and Advantages of Products or Services

The potential banker/investor wants to know exactly what you are going to sell, its proprietary features, if any, and its advantages and drawbacks.

Describe, in more detail than previously, the products or services that you sell or intend to sell and what needs they satisfy. Use diagrams, sketches, and pictures if these will aid understanding and heighten interest. Emphasize any distinctive features of your product or service by highlighting how it differs from what is currently on the market. State candidly each feature's advantage or disadvantage.

Describe any patents, trade secrets, or other proprietary features. Discuss any head start that you have or could have that would enable you to achieve a favored or entrenched position in your industry.

Also discuss any opportunities for the logical extension of your existing line or the development of related products or services. Investors like to know what you can do for an encore.

Market Research and Analysis

In this section of your plan, you should present enough facts to convince the reader that the market for your product or service is such that you can achieve your sales target in the face of competition. This is probably the most difficult section to do well. Yet it is also crucial, simply because choice of marketing strategies, size of work force and facilities, and requirements for inventory and receivables financing are all to be derived from sales forecasts. This section should be prepared before the rest of the plan and should be done very thoroughly.

Customers

Define the market clearly. Explain who are the major purchasers of your product or service, where they are, and why they buy. Discuss and indicate by rank order the significance of price, quality, service, personal contacts, and political pressures. When do they buy? Discuss how seasonal changes affect your business.

List some actual or potential customers who have purchased, expressed interest in, or placed an order for your product or service and indicate why. List any actual or potential customers who have dropped or shown no interest in your product or service, and explain why this was so. Explain what you are doing to overcome negative customer reaction.

Market Size and Trends

What is the size of the current total market for your product or service? This market should be determined by discussions with potential distributors, dealers, sales representatives, and customers. Any available published data should be reviewed as well. Do not rely solely on published information, as it is often inadequate and known to be so by industry insiders. Give the size of the total market in units as well as dollars. Be careful to include only the market you are in fact going after. If you intend to sell regionally, show the regional market size.

Describe the potential annual growth of the total market for your product or service. Market projections should be made for at least three years. Discuss in detail how the major factors such as industry trends, new technical developments, and new or changing customer needs are affecting market growth. Review previous market trends. Any differences between past and projected growth rates should be explained. If you are assuming that past trends will continue, say why. Be aware that overstatement of your market may discredit the rest of your proposal in the eyes of the reader. Information can be obtained from employer groups, accountants, industry studies, and magazines as appropriate.

Competition

Make a realistic assessment of the strengths and weaknesses of competitive products and services, and name the companies that supply them. State the data sources used to determine which products are competitive and the strengths of the competition. You should compare your products or services with your competitors' based on price, performance, service, warranties, and other pertinent features. A table can be an effective way of presenting such data.

Review the managerial and financial strengths and weaknesses of your competitors. Give your assessment of each competitor's capability in marketing, operations, and finance, and their recent trends in sales, market share, and profitability. If they are not doing well, explain why you expect to succeed.

Conclude this section by explaining why customers buy from your three or four key competitors. Then, from what you have presented about their operations, explain why you think that you can capture a share of their business—if that is how you plan to grow.

Entrepreneurs often know less about their competition than they should. This is a gross oversight. Professional lenders and investors are very wary of proposals that treat competition lightly.

Estimated Market Share and Sales

Identify any major customers who have made or are willing to make purchase commitments. Indicate the extent of these commitments. Estimate the share of the market and the sales in units and dollars that you think you can achieve. Base this estimate on your assessment of your customers and their acceptance of your product or service, your market size and trends, and the competition, their offerings, and their share of sales in the prior year. The growth of your sales and your estimated market share should be related to the growth of your industry and customers and to the strengths and weaknesses of your competitors. The data should be presented in tabular form, as the following example shows. If yours is an existing business, also indicate the total market, your market share, and sales for two prior years.

Sales and Market Share Data Over Two Years

	First Year				Second Year			
	Q1	Q2	Q3	Q4	Q1	Q2	Q3	Q4
Estimated total market								
Units								
Dollars								
Your estimated sales								
Units								
Dollars								
Your estimated market share								
Units								
Dollars								

The Marketing Plan

Your marketing plan should describe how you will achieve your sales target. It should include a description of your sales and service policies as well as pricing, distribution, and advertising strategies that you will use to achieve your goal. It should make clear what is to be done, how it will be done, and who will do it.

Marketing Strategy

A description of your marketing strategy (see "Marketing," Chapter 6) should include a discussion of the kinds of customers who will be targeted for an initial heavy selling effort and customers who will be sought for later selling efforts. It should include the methods of identifying and contacting specific potential customers, and the features of the product or service (quality, price, delivery, warranty) that will be emphasized to generate sales.

If the sales of your product or service are seasonal, discuss this and indicate any ideas you have for obtaining out-of-season sales.

Pricing

Many entrepreneurs, having convinced prospective investors that they have superior products, say they intend to sell them for less than their competitors. This makes a bad impression for two reasons. First, if your product is as good as you say it is, you should not have to undercut the competition. Second, if you use low prices as a marketing draw, you have no room for maneuvering. At least if you start at a higher price and costs run over budget, as they usually do, you have some leeway to come down. Price hikes are tougher to make stick than price cuts.

As you will see in Chapter 6, your pricing policy is one of the more important decisions you make. Your price must be right to penetrate your market, maintain your market position, and produce the profits you project. Devote enough time to considering a number of pricing strategies and convincingly present the one you select.

Discuss the prices to be charged for your product or service and compare your pricing policy with those of your major competitors. Explain how the price you set will enable you to do the following:

- Secure/increase acceptance of your business opportunity.
- Maintain and desirably increase your market share in the face of competition.
- Produce profits.

Justify any price increases over competitive items on the basis of newness, quality, warranty, and service. If your product is to be priced lower than your competitors' products, explain how you will do this without losing profitability.

Sales Tactics

Describe how you will sell and distribute your product or service. Do you or will you use your own sales force and distributors? Are there ready-made manufacturers' sales organizations selling related products that you already use or could use? If distributors or sales representatives are used, describe how they have been or will be selected and the areas they will cover. Discuss the margins to be given to retailers and wholesalers and commissions to be given to sales representatives. Compare them to your competitors' rates. Describe any special policies regarding items such as discounts and exclusive distribution rights.

If a direct sales force is being introduced, indicate how it will be organized and at what rate it will be built up.

Show the sales expected per salesperson per year and what commission incentive and/or salary he or she will receive. Explain how these figures compare to those of your competition.

Service and Warranty Policies

If your business will offer a product that will require service and warranties, indicate the importance of these to the customer's purchasing decision. Discuss your method of handling service problems.

Advertising, Public Relations, and Promotion

Describe the program you will use to bring your product to the attention of prospective customers. Indicate your plans for public relations, trade show participation, trade magazine advertisements, direct mailings, and the preparation of product sheets and promotional literature. If advertising will be a significant part of company expenses, present details of how and when these costs will be incurred.

Design and Development

If one of your products or services requires design and development before it is ready to go on the market, the nature and extent of this work should be fully discussed. The costs and time required to achieve a marketable product or service should be indicated.

Such design and development might be the engineering work necessary to convert a laboratory prototype to a finished product; the design of special tooling; the work of an industrial designer to make a product more attractive and saleable; or the identification and organization of manpower, equipment, and special techniques. Design and development might be the implementation of a service business—for example, the equipment, new computer software, and skills required for computerized credit checking.

Development Status and Tasks

Describe the current status of the product or service and explain what remains to be done to make it marketable. Describe briefly the competence or expertise that your business has, or will acquire, to complete this development. Indicate the type and extent of technical assistance that will be required, state who will supervise this activity within your organization, and give his or her experience in related development work.

Difficulties and Risks

Identify any major anticipated design and development problems along with ways of solving them. Discuss their possible impact on the timing of the market introduction of your product or service and on the cost of design and development.

Costs

Present and discuss a design and development budget. The costs should include labor, materials, consulting fees, and so on. Design and development costs are often underestimated. This can have a serious impact on cash flow projections. Accordingly, consider and perhaps show a 10- to 20-percent cost contingency. These cost data will become an integral part of the financial plan.

Production /Operations

The operations plan should describe the kind of facilities, space requirements, capital equipment, and labor force (part and full time) that are required to deliver the forecast quantities of the product or service (see "Business Hardware," Chapter 6). For a manufacturing business, discuss your policies regarding purchasing, "make or buy" decisions (which parts of the products will be purchased and which operations will be performed by your work force), inventory control, and production control. A service business should describe the appropriateness of location, lease of required equipment, and competitive productivity from a skilled or trained labor force.

The following discussion guidelines are general enough to cover both product and service businesses. Only those that are relevant to your business type should be used in preparing the business plan.

Geographic Location

Describe the location of the business. Discuss any advantages and disadvantages of the site in terms of wage rates, unions, labor availability, closeness to customers or suppliers, access to transportation, state and local taxes, and federal, state, and local laws, utilities, and zoning. For a service business, proximity to customers is generally a "must."

Facilities and Improvements

If the business already exists, describe the facilities currently used to conduct it. This should include plant and office space, storage and land areas, machinery, special tooling, and other capital equipment.

If you are starting up your own venture, describe how and when the necessary facilities to start production will be acquired. Discuss whether equipment and space will be leased or acquired (new or used) and indicate the costs and timing of such actions.

Indicate how much of the proposed financing will be devoted to plant and equipment.

Discuss how and when plant space and equipment will be moved or expanded to the capacities required to achieve future sales projections. Explain future equipment needs and indicate the timing and cost of any acquisitions. A three-year planning period should be used for these projections.

Production Strategies

Describe the manufacturing processes involved in producing your goods and any decisions with respect to subcontracting component parts rather than manufacturing them in-house. The "make or buy" strategy adopted should consider inventory financing, available labor skills, and other nontechnical questions as well as pure production, cost, and capability issues. Justify your proposed "make or buy" policy. Discuss any surveys you have completed of potential subcontractors and suppliers and name them.

Present a production plan that shows cost-volume information at various levels of operation, with breakdowns of applicable material, labor, purchased components, and factory overhead. Discuss the inventory required at various sales levels. These data will be incorporated into cash flow projections (see "Financial Plan," in this chapter and Chapter 6). Explain how any seasonal production loads will be handled without interrupting the business—for example, by building up inventory, using part-time help, or subcontracting the work.

Briefly describe your approach to quality, production, and inventory control. Explain what quality control and inspection procedures the company will use to minimize service problems and associated customer dissatisfaction.

Discuss how you will organize and operate your purchasing function to ensure that adequate materials are on hand for production, that the best price and payment terms have been obtained, and that raw materials and in-process inventory (and hence working capital) have been minimized.

Labor Force

Explain, exclusive of management functions, to what extent the local labor force has adequate skills for the needs of your business. Explain whether these skills are in sufficient quantity and quality (lack of absenteeism, productivity) to manufacture the product or supply your business's services to whatever standards of quality, time, and cost you have established. If the skills of the labor force are inadequate for the needs of your business, describe the kinds of training that you will use to upgrade the skills. Discuss how your business can provide and pay for such training and still offer a competitive product in both the short term (first year) and the long term (two to five years).

Management Team

The management team is the key to a successful business. Investors look for a committed management team with a balance of skills and experience in marketing, operations, and finance.

Accordingly, this section of the business plan will be of primary interest to potential investors and will significantly influence their investment decisions. It should include a description of the key members of the management team and their primary duties, the organizational structure, and the board of directors. The reputation and strength of at least one independent director will be critical when you seek financing or investors.

Organization

In a table, present the key management roles in the company and name the person holding each position.

If applicable, discuss current or past situations in which the key management people have worked together to indicate how their skills and personalities complement each other and result in an effective management team. If any key individuals will not be on hand at the start of the venture, specify when they will join the company or what you are doing to locate and secure commitments from such individuals. In a new business, it may not be possible to fill each executive role with a full-time person without burdening the venture's overhead. One solution is to use part-time specialists or consultants to perform some functions. If this is your plan, discuss it and indicate who will be used and when they will be replaced by a full-time staff member.

If the company is established and of sufficient size, an organization chart can be appended as an exhibit.

Executive Management Personnel

Describe the exact duties and responsibilities of each of the executive members of the management team. Include a brief (three- or four-sentence) statement of the career highlights of each individual to focus on accomplishments that demonstrate ability to perform the assigned role.

Complete résumés for each valued management member should be included here or as an appendix to the business plan. These résumés should stress the education, training, experience, and accomplishments of each person in performing functions similar to that person's role in the venture. Accomplishments should be discussed in terms of profit and sales improvement, labor productivity gains, reduced operating costs, improved product performance, and ability to meet budgets and schedules. When possible, name persons who can attest to such accomplishments, recognition, or rewards as pay increases and promotions.

Management Compensation and Ownership

The likelihood of obtaining financing for a start-up is small when the founding management team is not prepared to accept modest initial salaries. If you demand substantial salaries in excess of what you received at your prior employment, the potential lender or investor will conclude that your psychological commitment to the venture is a good deal less than it should be. In hard times, lenders and investors take a particularly dim view of actual or perceived abuses in the area of remuneration.

State the salary that is to be paid to each valued person and compare it with the salary received at his or her last independent job. Set forth the share ownership planned for the valued management team members, the amount of their equity investments (if any), and any performance-dependent options or bonus plans that are being considered. Mention any loans made to the company by management, indicating on what terms they were made and under what circumstances they can be converted to equity.

Board of Directors

Identify board members. Include a one- or two-sentence statement of each member's background to show how he or she can benefit the company and what investment (if any) has been made. Include the résumé of the independent board member, showing any other directorships.

Management Assistance and Training Needs

Describe candidly the strengths and weaknesses of your management team and board of directors. Discuss the kind, extent, and timing of any management training that will be required to overcome any weaknesses.

Supporting Professional Services

State the legal, accounting, public relations, advertising, banking, and other service organizations that you have selected for your venture. Supporting service organizations that are reputable and capable not only provide professional assistance but also can add significantly to the credibility of your business. In addition, properly selected professional organizations can help you establish good contacts in the business community, identify potential investors, and secure financing. Also, mention your mentor if you have one.

Overall Schedule

A schedule that shows the timing and interrelationship of the major events necessary to launch the business and realize its objectives is an essential part of a business plan. In addition to being a planning aid, a well-prepared and realistic schedule can be an extremely effective sales tool in raising money from potential bankers or investors. It also demonstrates the ability of the management team to plan for venture growth in a way that recognizes obstacles and minimizes risk.

Prepare, as a part of this section, a month-by-month schedule that shows the timing of activities such as product development, market planning, sales programs, and operations. Sufficient detail should be included to show the timing of the primary tasks required to accomplish each major goal.

Show the deadlines or milestones critical to the venture's success. These should include the following dates:

- Incorporation of the new business.
- Completion of prototypes (a key date because its attainment is a tangible measure of the company's ability to perform).
- Hiring of sales representatives.
- Signing up distributors and dealers.
- Ordering materials in sufficient quantities for full-time operation.
- Starting operation (another key date because it is related to the production of income).
- Receiving first orders.
- Making first sales and deliveries (an all-important date because it relates directly to the company's credibility and need for capital).
- Paying first accounts receivable (cash in).

The schedule should also show the following and their relation to the development of the business.

- Number of management personnel
- Number of operations personnel
- Additions to plant or equipment

Critical Risks and Problems

The development of a business has risks and problems, and the business plan invariably contains some implicit assumptions about them. Credibility can be undermined and finance endangered if negative factors are not openly addressed. On the other hand, identifying and discussing the risks in your venture demonstrates your skill as a manager and increases your credibility with a banker or investor. Taking the initiative to identify and discuss risks tells the lender or investor that you have thought about them and can handle them. Risks then tend not to loom as large black clouds in the lender's or investor's thinking.

Accordingly, identify and discuss the major problems and risks that you think you will have to deal with to develop your venture. Include a description of the risks relating to your industry, your company and its personnel, your product's market appeal, and the timing and financing of your start-up. Among the risks that might require discussion are

- Price cutting by competitors.
- Any potentially unfavorable industry-wide trends.
- Design or operating costs significantly in excess of estimates.
- Development schedule not met.
- Sales projections not achieved by target date.
- Difficulties or long lead times in procuring parts or raw materials.
- Difficulties in obtaining needed bank credit lines because of tight money.
- Larger-than-expected innovation and development costs to stay competitive.
- Lack of available trained labor.
- Change in the economy.
- Higher interest rates.

By no means comprehensive, this list is only indicative of the kinds of risks and assumptions involved.

Show which business plan assumptions or potential problems are most critical to the success of the venture. Describe your plans for minimizing the impact on the success of your venture of unfavorable developments in each risk area.

The Financial Plan

The financial plan is basic to any lender's or investor's evaluation of your business and should represent your realistic and best estimates of future operations. Its purpose is to indicate the financial potential of your enterprise and its capital needs. The financial plan should also serve as an operating plan for financial management of the business.

In developing your financial plan, three basic statements must be prepared.

- Profit and loss forecasts for three years
- Cash flow projections for three years
- Pro forma balance sheets at start-up, semiannually in the first year, and at the end of each of the first three years of operation

In the case of an existing business seeking expansion capital, balance sheets and income statements for the current and two prior years should be presented in addition to these finance projections.

After you have completed the preparation of the financial exhibits, briefly outline the important conclusions that can be drawn. This might include items such as the maximum cash requirement, the amount to be supplied by investors and debt, the level of profits as a percentage of sales, and how fast any borrowing is to be repaid.

Profit and Loss Forecast

The preparation of your business's projected income statements is the planning-for-profit part of your financial plan. The sales forecast is crucial to the earnings forecasts, as well as to other projections. The methods for developing sales forecasts have already been described in these guidelines, and the sales forecasts made there should be used here.

The following headings can be used in drawing up your profit and loss forecast for prospective investors.

Sales
> Less: Materials used
> Direct labor
> Manufacturing overhead (includes rent, utilities, fringe benefits, telephone)
> Other manufacturing expense, leased equipment, and so on
> Depreciation
> Total cost of goods sold

Gross profit (or loss)
> Less: Sales expenses
> General and administrative expenses, office supplies, accounting and legal services, management, and so on

Operating profit (or loss)
> Less: Other expenses (for example, interest)
> Profit (or loss) before taxes
> Income tax provision
> Profit (or loss) after taxes

The first year should show a monthly breakdown for each item. The second and third years should project quarterly figures. Figures for all three years should appear on a single sheet of ruled paper. Make sure the paper you use is large enough. (Tape two pages together if necessary.)

Once the sales forecasts are in hand, production costs (or operations costs for a service business) should be budgeted. The level of production or operation that is required to meet the sales forecasts and also to fulfill inventory requirements must be determined. The material, labor, service, and manufacturing overhead requirements must be developed and translated into cost data.

Sales expenses should include the costs of selling and distribution, storage, discounts, and advertising and promotion. General and administrative expenses should include management salaries, secretarial costs, and legal and accounting expenses. Manufacturing or operations overhead includes items such as rent, utilities, fringe benefits, and telephone.

Because of the importance of profit and loss projections, you should explain any assumptions that you made in their preparation. Such assumptions could include the amount allowed for bad debts and discounts, and sales expenses or general and administrative costs as a fixed percentage of costs or sales.

Cash Flow Forecast

For a new business, the cash flow forecast can be more important than the forecasts of profits because it details the amount and timing of expected cash inflows and outflows. Usually the level of profits, particularly during the formative years of a business, will not be sufficient to finance operating cash needs. Moreover, cash inflows do not match the outflows on a short-term basis. The cash flow forecast will show these conditions.

The cash flow forecast records *all* cash receipts and payments, including those that do not appear in the profit and loss statement—for example, the capital portion of loan payments. It does not record expenses that do not affect the flow of cash or profits, such as depreciation and provision for bad debts. In preparing the cash flow budget it is important to know or estimate both the *amount* of the income/expense to be received/paid and *when* it will occur. The purpose of this document is to predetermine the timing and size of shortfalls or surpluses, so that steps can be taken to arrange additional funds to be raised or invested as appropriate. If a continuous or increasing cash shortfall is forecast, a more permanent source of capital should be considered—for example, increased owners' equity or a longer term loan. The cash flow forecast should allow for actual income/payments to be inserted so that a comparison can be made with estimates.

Like the income statement, the cash flow analysis should cover three years, with the first year broken down into twelve monthly figures and the second and third years projected by quarters. Again, this analysis should be made on a single large sheet of ruled paper. The following headings can be used in preparing the analysis.

Bank balance: Opening (debit or credit)
ADD cash receipts
    Collection of debts/cash sales
    Miscellaneous receipts
    Bank loans
    Capital contributed
    Total receipts
LESS cash payments
    Credits
    Wages
    Manufacturing overhead
    Leased equipment
    Sales expenses
    General and administrative expenses
    Fixed asset purchases

Income tax

Loan interest @_____%

Loan repayments

Miscellaneous payments

Total disbursements

EQUALS cash surplus (or deficit)

Bank balance: Closing (debit or credit)

Given a level of projected sales and capital expenditures over a specified period, the cash flow forecast will highlight the need for, and timing of, additional financing and show you your peak requirements of working capital. You must decide how this additional financing is to be obtained, on what terms, and how it is to be repaid (see Chapter 4). Part of the needed financing will be supplied by yourself, by your family and friends, and by contacts and by professional investors; part by bank loans for one to five years; and the balance by short-term lines of credit from banks. This information becomes part of the final cash flow forecasts.

If the venture is in a seasonal or cyclical industry, in an industry in which suppliers require a new firm to pay cash, or if an inventory build-up occurs before the product can be sold and produce revenues, the cash flow forecast is crucial to the continuing operation of your business. A detailed cash flow forecast that you understand can enable you to direct your attention to operating problems without the distractions caused by periodic cash crises that you should have anticipated.

You should discuss the following assumptions: the timing of collection of debts, discounts given, terms of payments to your suppliers, planned salary and wage increases, anticipated increases in any operating expenses, seasonal characteristics of the business as they affect inventory requirements, and capital equipment purchases. Thinking about such assumptions when planning the operation of your business is useful for identifying issues that may later require attention if they are not to become significant problems.

Balance Sheet Forecasts

The balance sheet is used to show the assets required in the operation of your business and, through liabilities, how these assets are to be financed. Investors and bankers look to the projected balance sheet for information such as debt-to-equity ratios, working capital, current ratios, and inventory turnover. The lenders or investors will relate them to the acceptable limits required to justify future financings that are projected for the venture.

The following headings may be used to prepare the balance sheet forecasts.

ASSETS
    Current assets
    Cash
    Debts
    Stock
    Prepayments
Total current assets
Noncurrent assets
    Plant and equipment
    Less: Accumulated depreciation
    Net plant and equipment
    Land and buildings
    Other assets (identify)
Total assets
LESS LIABILITIES

Current liabilities
Loans
Credits
Accruals
Taxes
Other
Total current liabilities
Noncurrent liabilities
Long-term loans
Other liabilities (identify)
Total liabilities
EQUALS SHAREHOLDERS' (PARTNERSHIP) FUNDS
Paid-up capital
Retained profits
Total shareholders' (partnership) funds

Forecast balance sheets should be prepared at start-up, semiannually for the first year, and at the end of each of the first three years of operation.

Cost and Cash Flow Control

Your ability to meet your income and cash flow projections will depend on your ability to secure timely reports on, and effectively control, your operating costs. For this reason, bankers and investors will want to know what kind of cost-control systems you have or will use in your business. The financial plan should include a brief description of how you will design, install, and maintain systems for controlling costs and cash flows appropriate to the nature and size of your business, who will be responsible for getting cost data, how often cost data will be obtained, and how you will take action to reduce costs that are running higher than you expected.

Desired Financing

From your cash flow projections, summarize how much money is needed over the next three years to carry out the described development and expansion of your business. Indicate how much of this money you expect to obtain from your own resources and investors and how much you think you can borrow. Describe the kind (ordinary shares, convertible notes, debentures), the unit price, and the total amount of equity to be issued to investors. Also, show the percentage of the company that investors in this offering will hold after the offering is completed and what special rights they will have.

Capitalization

Use a table to show the names of your current shareholders and the number of shares each holds. Also indicate how many of your company's ordinary shares will remain authorized but unissued.

Use of Funds

Bankers and investors like to know how their money is going to be spent. Provide a brief description of how the capital raised will be used. Summarize as specifically as possible what amount will be used for such things as product development, capital equipment, marketing, and general working capital needs.

> **Case Study.** Wayne and Jenny were two friends who had known each other for some twenty years, since school. They had each worked for a number of graphic design and photographic studios for four or five years, and at the ripe old age of twenty-four they decided to go into business together.
>
> They had been doing quite nicely for about twelve months, with a very small office, a slide-making machine,

and a computer graphics package. The whole setup had cost them no more than $40,000. They developed a good client base and were basically running a small, tight, profitable business. They met regularly, and even went out to dinner every Thursday night without their spouses just to discuss business matters. The only problem they had was trying to get good staff.

They each wanted to buy their own homes and had decided to purchase two slide computer machines at a total cost of $300,000. This meant that, collectively, they were borrowing something like $800,000. They approached a company to prepare a business plan. With guidance from the company, they wrote their own plan with all the required elements: clearly stated goals and objectives; a great deal of market research, statistics, and studies; a marketing plan that was simple, logical, and easy to carry out; clear documentation of equipment, facilities, and location; very detailed cash flows and budgeting; and the exact financial requirements, with their contribution and the borrowing mix.

Although they knew the plan was ambitious, they submitted it to three financiers. One was a traditional bank, one was a finance company, and the other was a venture capital company. Within a week all three lenders had approved the financing and the managing director of the finance company sought aggressively to acquire a half-share in the business.

Jenny and Wayne were able to choose their financier and also had the option of taking on a partner who would inject capital, thereby reducing worry, risk, and interest. They deliberated over the next two days and came back with the decision, against much advice, to go it alone. They had made the right decision. Four years later they have stuck rigidly to their plan; they haven't made any major changes or increased commitments. They are achieving the profits they said they would and they are rapidly reducing their debt. They are still meeting every Thursday night; they are still reviewing their figures; they know exactly what their costs are and their break-even point is. And they have their staff problem under control.

Presenting Your Plan

Presenting the business plan that you have so carefully and painstakingly prepared should not be a daunting experience. On the contrary, it should be your moment of glory, your reason to feel proud.

As mentioned earlier, a number of people should be presented with a copy of the plan, but this section will focus on prospective lenders. Some straightforward rules apply (and also hold true for potential investors).

First, before making contact with your chosen financier, make sure you understand every aspect of the plan. If you have prepared it according to the above guidelines, this shouldn't cause any problems, unless it contains difficult financial information. If an accountant prepared it, perhaps you should invite him or her to join you at the meeting. Familiarize yourself with every word and every figure to such an extent that you will not need to refer to the report during your interview.

Next, find out from your lending institution who has the relevant authority. Explain the purpose of your intended visit and make an appointment to see that person. In advance of your visit, send a copy of your plan with an agenda for discussion.

Be on time for your interview. Dress neatly, in a suit or equally businesslike outfit. (Jeans are definitely out.) Even if wearing such attire is not usual for you, show flexibility in adapting to the conventions of different environments, in this case that of the commercial lender. On the other hand, don't overdress. Your aim is to convey a professional and capable image. Consider having your spouse or business partner accompany you to the interview to show support and commitment.

In addition to your copy of the business plan, take all available financial statements and projections, having had these checked by your accountant (or having had them prepared by your accountant if you don't have the skills). Also take any relevant statistics, survey data, maps, and analyses and offer copies to the bank's representative. Let the bank's (or lender's or investor's) representative do most of the talking to start with, giving you time to relax and prepare yourself. When you do speak, do so slowly and clearly. Don't be vague or overpowering. Be enthusiastic, but don't push for a decision. The lender or investor will need time to think about the interview and to some extent will be guided by your performance at it. Inspire him or her with your confidence and your ability to run the business, repay the loan, and return a profit on the investment.

Behave professionally. Show that you are serious and capable of running an efficient and profitable business. Treat your prospective lender or investor with respect. When you present your business plan, you are selling your business, your professionalism, your expertise, and your commitment. In exchange, you are looking to buy their product—money. The first impression that you create as a person will be a lasting one. Conduct yourself with your lenders and investors just as you do with your customers and creditors.

It is very important that you be honest and communicate openly. Be realistic: Don't ignore the negative side of the picture. Be frank. The lender or investor will place great store on your honesty, so answer any questions candidly and completely. You can be certain that you won't get a loan if you raise suspicion that you are holding back information. Apart from protecting your own reputation and your long-term relationship with the lender or investor, you want to enhance your chances of obtaining further loans or investment funds or being able to come back later if the first application is declined.

If your request is declined, find out why and what you have to do to correct the reason for being turned down. This will enable you to revamp your business plan to meet the criteria given. Don't give up, even after three or four rejections. If you have properly prepared your plan and believe in it, you needn't feel anxious, particularly when money is tight and the bankers take a long time to make up their minds and impose increasingly stringent requirements. Unfortunately, in these hard times many good bankers have been shifted into recovery because of the increased number of bad debts, or they have been transferred from branch to branch to ensure that they maintain their detachment. The banks' senior executives are putting a lot of pressure on bankers with regard to the high number of nonperforming loans. That is why they may be slightly negative at the moment and also why you need to shop around.

Just keep making approaches until you find the ideal mix with a lender or investor who suits you. Two of the biggest companies in the United States—Digital and Research and Development—were turned down by many lenders and investors before they got going.

Remember, a good business plan is one that raises money. A bad plan does not attract investors and does not raise money. That idea is simple enough, but remember that a good plan does not necessarily create a good business. A good plan may raise money, but the business may still fail. However, a bad plan almost always leads to a failed business. To succeed, you need a good plan plus a good business.

4

RAISING MONEY

Besides salaries, financing is often the major cost to a small business. When interest rates are relatively low, this cost can usually be carried without too much effort. But when rates are high, financing costs tend to decrease the fair return for efforts or even cause businesses to go broke.

Wherever possible, it is best to avoid using other people's money to finance your business. Ideally, the business should be self-financing—that is, the profit should be its source of financing. When you are making profits, you are putting money back into your business, increasing your working capital (stock, debts), and increasing your profits in the future. Money earned by the business is the best and cheapest source of financing. It does not incur interest and does not have to be repaid. It's totally controllable—it can't be taken from you—and you don't have to sign any guarantees or put up any security for it. If your business is just beginning and is expanding rapidly, you are forced to maintain an increased sales volume to meet the increasing overhead costs. Often a slower rate of progress is better, making costs easier to control and operations more profitable even if the total sales are down, thus minimizing the need to borrow. After all, you should be interested only in net profit and not expansion for the sake of expansion.

However, your ability to expand or to take advantage of an opportunity will often depend on an injection of funds from external sources. Even if you have funds available from internal sources, it might still be a good idea to start looking for outside money long before you have fully used all of your own. If you do this, do you want equity capital from investors, debt capital from a finance company or bank, or perhaps both?

Equity capital means selling off part of your business by taking on a partner or selling shares. Before investing, investors will want to read your business plan. Let's say your business is worth $400,000 net (including stock and goodwill), and you are prepared to divest yourself of 40 percent in order to retain the majority of the shares. The contribution from investors would then be $160,000 (40% × $400,000). For that capital to remain in the business, you would need to lend that money back to the business on agreed terms, because really you are selling shares that belonged to you. When you do this, there is less pressure to repay the funds. However, possible disincentives are that you lose exclusive control of your business and you may introduce the partnership problems discussed in Chapter 2.

When considering borrowing, you will need to take into account three factors: cost, availability, and terms. Shop around for the deal that suits you in all these respects. Make sure the term of the loan matches the purpose for which it is intended. Always borrow short to invest short and borrow long to invest long; to borrow short and invest long is one of the easiest paths to the business grave.

A line of credit from a bank is the most popular type of finance sought by small businesses because it is the most flexible. Although you will be charged a line fee that is tied to the approved limit of the credit, you will pay interest only on the amounts of money you use. The rate will vary according to the market and the status of your business.

The following chart is a guide to types and main sources of funds.

Short-Term Debt Finance	Medium-Term Debt Finance	Long-Term Debt Finance	Owner's/ Investors' Equity Capital
Up to 3 years (including temporary working capital; bridging finance; funds to meet seasonal fluctuations; finance for short-term assets)	3-10 years (including finance for assets with medium-term life such as plant and machinery, general working capital, line of credit funding)	More than 10 years (including finance for long-life assets such as buildings, corporate acquisitions)	(including permanent capital such as for technological innovation, development and expansion, refinancing of loans)
Commercial banks	Commercial banks	Commercial banks	Family/friends
Savings banks	Savings banks	Savings banks	Accountants/ lawyers
Finance companies	Finance companies	Finance companies	Life insurance companies
		Church groups	Retirement funds
		Life insurance companies	Stockbrokers
		Other insurance companies	Venture capital companies
		Retirement funds	Private individuals
		Debt raising	

Excessive dependence on a bank line of credit (in principle, repayable on demand) is dangerous, particularly in the eyes of other prospective suppliers of financing. If you do have a line of credit, make sure you use it, even if you have to swap checks back and forth. Don't sit on your approved limit, or it will be considered a poor debt and the bank might either force you to pay it back or exchange it for a higher, fixed-interest loan with additional security. Cyclical requirements can be serviced by commercial bills on which interest is charged up front and that are repayable in full on maturity. Another form of finance is a short-term loan—say, for twelve to eighteen months. Long-term funding comes from various sources, such as long-term business loans. Security is usually required against all bank financing, and suitability depends on your cash flow.

Remember that there is no point in changing your borrowing from bank to bank because it may cost you in processing and legal fees as well as in time spent negotiating, meeting, and preparing documentation. The banks are wise to such maneuvering, anyway.

In all your business dealings, never lose sight of the twin specters of undercapitalizing and overtrading. These two problems often go together because, although they do not mean quite the same thing, they stem from a common source.

The trading entity is rather like an upside-down pyramid with the sales represented by the upper horizontal line and the capital by the bottom point. If the point is too weak to support the remainder, the business will topple over into bankruptcy or the liquidation courts.

Undercapitalization can lead to inadequate supplies of materials and consequent disruption to production and delivery, lost opportunities, and expensive buying procedures. An overambitious business may follow a policy of going for increased sales volume, and overtrading is likely to occur. Outside borrowing is increased until a stage is reached in which inability to meet interest and capital repayments forces a showdown.

Never allow your business to reach even the edge of these deadly shores. One way to check on safety is to calculate the capital ratio, that is, the ratio of borrowed funds to your own money. Every business is different, and circumstances have some bearing on individual cases. Even so, the ideal ratio for a business is usually determined by the norm for that particular industry. In general, the greater the degree of risk attached to a particular type of business, the lower the desirable capital ratio. A sound balance sheet usually shows a capital ratio of not more than 1:2; that is, your equity is at least twice borrowings. For small businesses the ratio 1:1 would be the maximum capital ratio that should be attempted, except where there are temporary or special factors.

When a business's capital ratio approaches the higher end of its normal range, this should be taken as a danger signal, a strong sign that a further equity injection is becoming desirable, if not essential. Neither the lender's nor the owner's interests are served by too much outside financing. A business in a highly leveraged position applying to borrow funds for further expansion can expect the lender to require an injection of the borrower's own money or equity financing as a condition of lending, quite possibly of a greater amount than that being lent. In the eyes of the lender, the equity base represents the owner's commitment to the business, and the greater the commitment, the more likely the lender's willingness to help. Lack of equity or one's own money in a small business would normally necessitate personal guarantees by shareholders and directors.

The chief dangers of high capital ratios are quite simple: The burden of interest payments and any scheduled debt repayments will become too great in relation to the earnings and cash flow available to meet them. Also, a business with such a limited cash equity base will be unable to cushion or absorb the impact of suddenly adverse trading conditions. One useful test of the capacity to service debt repayments is whether the net trading profits before interest and tax cover the total of all interest charges at least twice over.

You should note that government restrictions apply to the seeking of investors and equity. While this topic is not relevant to this book, it is critical that you understand it. Seek advice from your accountant and/or lawyer.

Romancing the Bankers

When you approach your bank—be it to borrow or to invest— always show courtesy and respect. Don't turn up with your figures on scraps of paper. Your banker is a busy person, and you will be welcome only if you make an effort to communicate clearly and efficiently.

When considering applications for financing, banks are interested in three things. First, they look at your *reputation*, your track record—how you have conducted yourself in the past in dealing with lending and investing institutions. Your reputation is also your standing in the business community among your peers and competitors.

Second, they look at *cash flow* from the business—your ability to repay the loan—that should be included in your business plan. Indicate clearly how you will be able to afford the commitments you are taking on; whether they are interest commitments, repayments of dividends, or share of profit to potential investors; and how comfortably you will be able to do that while at the same time maintaining your business growth and your lifestyle. Banks and investors don't want to have bad debts; they prefer to make sure that you can pay them back or you can return a profit to them on their invested dollars. Remember that bankers are paid a wage that is contingent upon their performance, and that performance has a number of criteria. Obviously, any bad debts or bad loans affect their performance and chances for promotion. On the other hand, good loans, good debts, and good customers enhance their incomes. They like to see you actively transacting on your account, depositing into and withdrawing from your credit line.

Finally, banks are interested in *security*. Banks consider some or all of the following as security or collateral: mortgages on real estate, floating charges on the assets of your business, bills of sale on the fittings and plant owned by the business, and guarantees of different types. In the case of a company, bankers will usually request real estate security and personal guarantees from directors. They may also seek a charge over the company's assets. Banks make their own valuations of assets and determine their lending on that basis. In hard times, though, most lenders will look only at "bricks and mortar," and then they cut back on lending values. Other assets that can be used for security include collectible debts, stock (of which they take the low value), and life insurance policies with cash surrender values. Security to be offered must be clearly documented and listed. If it is property, provide the bank with all the necessary information, such as the volume and folio numbers, the address, even the current valuation (although lenders will still do their own appraisals).

A major part of romancing the bankers is to keep in touch. Don't just walk away after you have your line of credit, your loan, or your money invested. Keep in touch on a regular basis—at least every three to four months, more frequently if your business is going through tough times or rapid growth. Keep a close eye all day every day on your cash projections, amendments, and so forth. If you need more credit or money for the business, or if things are going to get tight, talk to your banker in advance. Provide him or her with cash flows and projections so that you can both predict what your needs will be. How much better it would be if a note in the bank's file were to read: "Mrs. X telephoned to warn me of a check that she had drawn that might take her $1,000 over the agreed limit. I told her this would be all right," rather than "I had to telephone Mrs. X to tell her the account was $1,000 over the limit. I warned her that I might not pay the check next time."

> **Case Study.** Rosemary was in the convention business. She had worked for a number of companies before going into her own business, so her eyes were wide open about human follies and weaknesses. Rosemary had a good accountant, one she had taken time to select. She worked strictly according to the business plan prepared for her and always stayed in touch with her accountant and her banker, informing them of all developments in her business. Over the years she had socialized with her banker and established trust; she had honored all her commitments; and she made payments on all her loans when they were due, if not before. She had a good credit history. However, she had hit cash flow problems. When the time came for her to take on a major new project, she had to consider a rapid expansion of staff and computer facilities. And when she asked for the money to do this, the bankers couldn't refuse.

Remember that a great deal of emphasis is placed on the integrity and management ability of the owners of any business. This can tip the scales in a marginal application for finance or investment. It is logical that the larger the amount of money required, the more professional your application for credit must be. You should familiarize yourself with the different types of loans, such as lines of credit. You should know what term of loan you want and what your business can afford. If your business is a strong cash generator, you can afford a reduction of the loan and payment of interest on a line of credit within a relatively short period of time. However, the term of the loan should be compatible with the cash flow forecast of the business. Quite often it is advisable to organize an interest-only loan, say for the first two years, before principal repayments are made, if this is what matches the cash flow.

Deal with the negatives. If you ignore them in your plan, readers will wonder whether you are telling the whole story. Be aware of the flaws and weaknesses of your plan and be armed to address them clearly and concisely. Also, anticipate any other negatives that the lender might raise. He or she might ask about your business's ability to meet its sales targets, especially in a poor economic environment. You will need to prove that these conditions have been taken into account and that the figures have been conservatively calculated.

To recap, the main things that lenders and investors look for are track record, cash flow, and security. The relative importance of those three will vary. In hard times, security tends to receive priority, then cash flow, then track record, but all three must stack up if you are to secure any money from the bank or an investor. Other criteria for the lender are likely to include the following:

- How much equity is the owner putting up?
- What form or amount of security is being offered? What proportion does this represent of the total funds required?

- What is the income-generating ability of the activity? In other words, what is its viability?

- Is the market healthy and growing? Are changes expected in the market trend? The lender will often inspect the proposed site for the business and the situation of competition in the area.

- What is the character or integrity of the applicant? What previous track record does he or she have in the field? Loan officers and managers heavily weight an impression of integrity and genuineness.

- Does the applicant appear over-enthusiastic and under-researched? Is there an appropriate attitude of commitment, ideally demonstrated by a high equity contribution?

- What is the applicant's prior industry track record?

- How much is required? Is it sufficient or excessive?

- What is the business classification? Is it capital intensive, involving purchase of plant and equipment and requiring long-term finance—for example, manufacturing, industry, transport, garages? Or is it labor intensive, involving high start-up costs, rental, stock and wages, and predominantly short-term finance—for example, video rental outlets?

- What is the present state of technology? Will the equipment become obsolete? Also, what is the state of industrial relations within the industry?

- Is the business a new venture, not taking on any established concern? If so, all criteria will need to be scrutinized more closely.

- Will the business be a private company? If so, will the directors sign guarantees?

- What is the nature of the product or service? What roles do seasonal factors play?

- Is the applicant impressive? Is the application well thought out? Obviously, bankers and loan officers have good instincts for quality in this regard.

- In the opinion of small business associations, how viable is the proposal?

- What are the applicant's credit ratings, value of accounts, and connections?

- What is the standard of the accounting information given? Audited accounts are especially welcome even if statements contain a disclaimer.

Finally, and incidentally, the banker or investor will be interested to learn of any peripheral advantages to be derived from approving your loan or accepting your investment. For example, should any members of your family bank elsewhere, or perhaps at a different branch of the same bank, their business might be transferable. Look for other business to give the banker, such as foreign exchange operations and so forth.

Creative Money Raising

Entrepreneurs in need of money tend to think automatically of borrowing. But external financing can also be obtained in the form of good old creditors. Most creditors allow at least one month's credit for purchases. So it is usually possible to rely on accommodation from this source to the amount of your material and other purchases. However, the amount owing to creditors tends to fluctuate during the month, and from month to month, due to variation in the level of purchases. You will, therefore, need to allow for these fluctuations.

You will have to build up a good reputation with the creditor before he or she will let you extend your terms. It would not be wise to extend payments beyond the arrangement made, as this practice leads to loss of goodwill and loss of profit from failure to benefit from discounts. If you are going to use creditors and need extended time for payment, make sure you communicate in advance. Customers or debtors should also not be overlooked as a source of debt capital. If your product or service is important to them, they may be willing to fund your business expansion by prepaying for your goods or services, or at least paying cash or paying earlier to help you through your rough patch.

Finance companies are another source of external financing. They provide commercial construction and consumer loans for purposes such as purchase of equipment, leasing of plant or motor vehicles, or even working capital. They also finance accounts receivable as well as other types of loans.

The sale of accounts receivable, or factoring, can assist your company through difficult times. For some businesses, factoring may be the only source of financing available, while for others it may be a stepping stone to a more sophisticated management or (more likely) failure. Factoring tends to be extremely expensive and very hard to repay. Only infrequently have businesses come out of factoring better off.

Leasing plant and equipment is widely used as a means of obtaining capital resources for a business. The usual method is that the lessor purchases the plant from a supplier and then leases it to you for an agreed period. Of course the real advantage of leasing is that it conserves your capital. But it can be extremely expensive, and you lose ownership of the property. Don't do it just because it is tax deductible, because it still has a large cash flow effect. Also, in purchasing capital equipment of any kind, it is always advisable to negotiate for trade-in allowances on old equipment, assuming this is appropriate.

A question often asked is what is the best way for a business to finance a car. There is usually a preconception that leasing is best, but this has come from car salespeople motivated by commissions on finance brokerage and the deduction of interest payable on the cars that are on the lot. Leasing is also often marketed as providing the best tax deduction, and while taxes are certainly an important consideration, they should be the last. Leasing isn't always the best arrangement, especially if you can't afford it in the first place. You might be better off buying a second-hand car rather than leasing a new car. Remember the golden rule: self and family first, cash flow second, tax deduction last.

Another way to enhance your cash flow is to reorganize your business and derive funds from the sale of any assets that are not earning adequate returns, such as surplus stock. This money can then be injected into more rewarding parts of the business to make profits.

If you have a commitment to expand your business or to replace existing assets, you should retain a high percentage of your business profits for these purposes. If, on the other hand, you are not expanding or replacing existing assets, there will still be the need for funds from retained profits. Remember, you need to finance not only real expansion but also expansion due to inflation.

Look at the possibility of putting your idle funds to work by cash budgeting and by eliminating the amounts kept for immediate needs. The essence of effective cash management is to keep idle dollars at an absolute minimum and any surplus working for you, earning interest.

Another way to free up funds is to keep tight credit control—keep your debts to a minimum. (The importance of collecting promptly from your debtors is dealt with in detail in Chapter 5.) Any stock you have on hand should be closely looked at. Do you need that much stock? Can buying be postponed until after the end of the month? Delaying purchases for a few days may give you an extra thirty days to pay. Stock is unsold sales. You would do better buying little and often rather than lots and seldom.

> **Case Study.** Some entrepreneurs even generate cash by taking on a second job. George was a fellow who has a furniture factory. He had about twelve staff members and, during a rough period, he planned to do the work of three people to keep paying the others. He was advised to go back to his trade as an electrician and cut back his staff to a minimum. That is what he did, and he is now back on track.

An alternative form of financing is the sale and lease-back of existing properties. This procedure enables the owner of a freehold property to sell the property to a financial institution, such as a life insurance company, then take a long lease on that property. The owner thereby realizes the value of the property in hard cash and can use the funds to run the business. Sometimes an agreement to repurchase the property at the end of the lease period can be arranged.

Credit cards are another form of short-term finance for small businesses. Most financial institutions provide major credit cards. They are convenient but expensive.

Often there is talk about overseas money, with interest rates making a very attractive comparison with those at home. However, when the dollar is at high levels, overseas borrowing presents some risks. Over and above the interest charges, a loan will cost a lot more to repay if the exchange rate fluctuates downward during its term. You can protect yourself from this by taking out insurance called hedging.

However, a true hedge will only bring the two interest rates into line and will involve a further cost.

You should shop around when you are thinking of financing. Consider all of the alternatives. Weigh the costs, the terms, the security required, and the appropriateness for your business. You will be amazed how much interest rates will vary.

It is also advisable during good times to line up sources of financing that you may not use, or to borrow even though you don't need to just for the sake of establishing a credit rating. As we all know, it is very difficult to borrow money when times are tough, but a good track record certainly helps.

In summary, you should keep the following factors in mind when seeking money.

- Maximize the use of money from within the business itself.

- Control expenses, improve stock turnover, make every effort to become and stay liquid, and check the gross profit ratio. Many cash problems are only the evidence of other problems within the business.

- If you decide that you really do need outside funds, carefully budget all requirements to make sure you use the most satisfactory source of funds.

- Remember that the state of the money market determines how you can best meet your requirements.

- Understand that short-term financing should meet short-term needs. Bridge loans and lines of credit, whether from banks or similar institutions, are satisfactory ways of satisfying your short-term needs, such as those caused by seasonal fluctuations, stock buildups, major works in progress, or needs for working capital.

- At all times preserve the borrowing potential for your business. In the end, you will be bound by the resources that you can command and your ability to service them.

- When you are looking to raise external financing, shop around.

- Finally, always have available more than one source of financing—more than one bank, more than one finance company.

PART TWO

BEING THERE

5

INGREDIENTS FOR SUCCESS

Here are some important factors for ensuring the success of your small business, some of which have already been mentioned in this book.

- Lead from the front. Lead by example.
- Don't fool yourself. (Who are you trying to impress and why?) Don't let your ego take over.
- Plan long term. Be in for the marathon, not the sprint.
- Employ and associate with only the best people, especially those in management and administration. Make sure your staff members are more intelligent or better qualified than you. Recognize that they are an asset to the business and pay them accordingly.
- Have more-than-adequate capital backing.
- Formulate monthly profit-and-loss balance figures. Compare them with the budget. Critically analyze cash flow. Always watch the bottom line—the profit line.
- Avoid internal politics.
- Don't trust anyone without concrete reasons for doing so.
- Service your clientele. The client comes first, last, and in between.

- Constantly listen, study, and learn.
- Avoid the legal minefield.
- Commit early to quality; start with the best or what you think is going to be the best.
- Don't do things by half; don't accept second best.
- Dot your *i*'s, cross your *t*'s. Do things properly the first time.
- Don't grow too quickly.
- Concentrate on cash flow. Ensure that it is always constant and sufficient to maintain the fuel you burn as your small business engine goes along. Make sure you have enough cash to start off with, that you don't go into business having to borrow a lot of money. Always be frugal; always be conservative.
- Build your business.
- Diversify in all senses—in terms of income sources, suppliers, staff, borrowing sources, and investment.
- Look after your suppliers; pay them on time and make them your allies and your friends.
- Ensure that all your products and services are of the highest quality. Let their quality be your best advertisement.
- Constantly watch your overhead, particularly in a hard economic environment. Don't let a little bit of cash flow and profit get to you. Don't suddenly go out and have that overseas vacation or buy that luxury car.
- Be organized, plan, and keep track with good book-keeping so you have accurate information on how your business is performing.
- Don't fall into the habit of "lazy marketing"— advertising in the newspapers or going to a trade show

and exhibiting your products. Get out there in the marketplace, wear out your shoes, knock on doors, and make phone calls. Keep going until it hurts. Get bored, because when you are getting bored you are usually getting cash flow and, it is hoped, profits.

- Don't be too soft. Many businesses have been exploited because their owners were too nice. Know when to say "No." It is the most difficult word. Don't be swayed by people trying to sell you stock lines or things at a discount. Remember that stock is cash, and you need that cash for your business.

- Manage your time efficiently, bearing in mind that you are probably the main, if not the only, income producer in your business.

Case Study. Four men combined to take over a retail wine and wholesale bottling business. Each of them was an expert in his own field. Barry was marketing manager of a timber production and distribution business, and he was also a shareholder. Paul was a wine connoisseur and journalist. Gavin was a successful accountant. Mark was an expert marketing and public relations consultant.

When they took over the business, it had not been very successful. It had cash flow and profit problems. You would think that the combination of these four experts would turn the business around or at least maintain it at its existing position of breaking even or making a small profit. Not so.

None of the four gave the venture the attention it deserved. Each took a part-time attitude, concentrating on personal business affairs to the detriment of the joint venture. Of course, they had lots of meetings and made lots of plans and, granted, their intentions were noble; but they did not manage to achieve anywhere near the prosperity that was possible. Within two years the business had been sold at a loss and, what's worse, all the partners had fallen out with each other.

The Basics: Sell, Profit, Collect

Successful management of a business is a complex process that is dealt with in detail in Chapter 6. However, of supreme importance, and therefore worth dealing with in advance, is the principle that lies at the heart of all successful commercial enterprise: sell, profit, and collect.

Sell

If you don't *sell* your product or service, nothing else will happen. The best accounting systems, the best products, the best staff, and the best location are meaningless unless a sale is made or a deal is closed because, otherwise, you won't have any cash flow and you won't be able to pay your bills. However, despite its importance, don't get carried away with the sale as an end in itself. It's not the end; it's only the beginning.

Profit

Every service provided and every sale made must be at a *profit*, otherwise the exercise is pointless. Because of its association with the excesses of big business, profit has become a dirty word. But, restored to its original meaning, profit is merely a healthy measure of the effectiveness of management in satisfying the wants of the consumer. It is no coincidence that many of the firms that make good profits also offer customers the best value for their money.

Knowing what your costs are and that you will make a profit takes the anxiety and worry out of your business. You should know exactly (per day, per week, per month) what sales you need to make in order to cover all your costs—in other words, what your break-even point is. As an employee of your own business, you should include in your costs what you would be paid in another business, then add a profit margin for the risk and the return on your money invested. Add up your overhead—rent, wages (yours and your staff's)—interest on money borrowed, dividends to anyone who has invested in your business, stock, and purchases. Sell at an amount above that to make a profit. Then you can reinvest in the business and grow to the level that you want in accordance with your business plan.

As mentioned in Chapter 3, one of the biggest mistakes most people make when they first start off in business is that they feel compelled to undercut their competitors. But pricing is a matter of confidence—in your product, in your service, and in yourself. Most businesses offer a service or product that rests on years or decades of experience, and this experience should be factored into the price.

There is a story about Picasso in a restaurant: A woman asked the great man to scribble something on a napkin, saying she would be happy to pay whatever he felt it was worth. Picasso obliged and said, "That will be $10,000."

The astonished woman replied, "But you did that in thirty seconds."

"No," Picasso said, "it took me forty years to do that."

Collect

Finally, having sold your product or service at the appropriate profit, you must now *collect* your money. There is no point in a sale or provision for profit unless you get paid. Perhaps it should be the first consideration—don't make sales to customers who cannot assure you of payment. Money owed to your business is effectively a type of unsecured loan. If you, in turn, have borrowed money from the bank to finance your business, it is costing you interest not to collect what is owed to you. When money is in short supply, as it is now, it is more important than ever that you run a tight ship in collecting from your debtors and repaying your creditors. Otherwise, the banks could close down your business by deciding to call in your line of credit or other loans.

Accounts receivable or debt lists should be kept up to date and arranged in order of size of debt. Imagine the impact if your largest debtor announced its liquidation to you tomorrow. Apart from the profit portion of the debt, what would be the out-of-pocket loss to your business? Would you be able to sustain such a loss? Study the spread of your risks. Do you have a large number of small debtors or perhaps a heavy reliance on a hard core or just a few? Examine the aging of your receivables ledger. A well-maintained ledger system will give you a monthly report of receivables split between those that are current and those thirty, sixty, and ninety days or more overdue. What percentage of your total receivables is in each category, in both number and dollar value?

You must also examine the policies you use as a basis for giving credit. If the profit margin is low, the out-of-pocket loss in bad debts will be high, so there is every justification for keeping the terms very tight. (They should always be tight anyway.) Examine the steps you use to assess new accounts. The information you seek will include account name and address; whether it is a company, partnership, sole proprietor, or trust; reference from a bank or another supplier; years in business; names and addresses of directors; and credit limit requested. Don't be lazy in this area. Do your homework and make sure you check out the potential customer thoroughly. Visit any larger potential customers worth considering. This can help you gain an insight into the business. Points to consider would include the morale of the business, appraisal of the proprietor, level of business activity, office system, quality of equipment, and so on. Sales personnel are generally less inclined to be critical in their evaluation of new and existing clients, for obvious reasons. Hence the need for an independent review.

In some industries it is possible to reduce the risk of extending credit by obtaining directors' guarantees on company accounts, a cash price with an order or upon delivery of goods, your retention of title to goods after delivery or until payment is made, trade credit insurance, or, in some cases, the taking of security such as a bank guarantee or a charge over an asset of the customer. Most of these will not be available on a normal trade account, but if the stakes are high, you should adopt all or some of these securities. Always remember that the extension of credit carries with it the need for providing additional cash, the cost of which is interest, whether paid or foregone. (This is called the opportunity cost.)

Dealing with slow payers should be planned well in advance and should follow a set procedure. It may involve the issuing of an "account rendered" statement followed by demands for payment, reference to a credit agency or lawyer, or simply presenting in person. Among small business customers, those responsible are usually the owners, who should be easy to identify and locate. Be positive in your collection effort and remember what was already mentioned about friendship: Be friends with your customers and they are more likely to pay you promptly.

Your operation's literature and invoices must make very clear your payment terms—seven, fourteen, thirty, or sixty days. In the past, sixty days was the normal trading term, but nowadays you should insist on payment at least within thirty days. If your debtors haven't paid by the due date, they should be closely monitored, probably weekly, and followed up with statements, reminder letters, and telephone calls.

When attempting to collect an overdue account, obtain a specific and personal promise for payment. Write in your diary the promise and the name of the person who made it. Not only will this procedure allow you to keep track and collect more easily, it will give you more confidence in approaching the debtor when following up on a broken promise. Do not believe anyone in an accounts payable department who tells you that the payments are computer controlled and that the process cannot be interrupted or circumvented. Any company, large or small, has the capability to handwrite checks.

Cash discounts can be used effectively. By giving discounts, where applicable, to prompt payers, you are rewarding your reliable customers and encouraging them to continue trading with you. This is a positive approach and eliminates bad feelings. You should first calculate the cost of this discount to your business and show the applicable rates in the official price list given to every eligible customer.

In hard times there is no point in being soft with slow payers. If someone owes your business money and your reminders fall on deaf ears, just go and sit in his or her office until you get a result. If embarrassment doesn't work, go right in with the legal documents. Get in and get your money, and always bank it on the date of receipt.

You might also consider selling on credit cards. At least you will be guaranteed payment by a fixed time after the sale. But make sure you build their charges into your costs. Another way to ensure payment is to take security from your customers in the form of personal guarantees.

Most importantly, supply only customers who have a proven capacity to pay. Do a credit check—have the customer fill in all the necessary information, then call and verify it. Don't rely on bank opinion; it's not enough. Most businesses have some bad debt. Prospective customers seeking credit should offer trade and bank references that should always be checked thoroughly. Inquiries should be made with local employee groups. Bank credit checks are invariably vague, but if you have a close relationship with your own banker, he or she will probably be able to interpret and expand on them for you.

> **Case Study.** Evan's father had spent thirty years building up his own electrical business. Business had flourished, even though Evan's father did not have sophisticated reporting systems. The reasons were basic: He had a grip on all his costs, never borrowed money, had loyalty from his employees, serviced his customers, and collected his money. On the last day of each month Evan's father would work late and then drive to the post office to mail out the invoices for prompt payment.
>
> Eventually, Evan took over business. But he didn't have quite the same attitude about cash. He was more interested in electrical equipment than in management. Evan also had enormous family troubles that he anguished over and that distracted him from the business. He then started to drink excessively. He didn't dot the *i*'s and cross the *t*'s, and he didn't pay attention to cash flow.
>
> His business has recently collapsed. He couldn't even sell it, so excessive were the liabilities. For all his efforts and generosity in handing over a business worth $3 million, Evan's father is barely going to have enough money to retire on. The lessons here are many.

A perfectly good business could come unglued due to the failure of its major clients. It could also have a preference claim brought against it. If a debtor who is having difficulties pays you and then goes into liquidation or becomes bankrupt, the administrator can reclaim the money if it is considered to be a preferential payment. One way to protect yourself against those types of situations is to know your customers. Another way, if you have particularly large customers or large sales, is to try to get a letter of credit, which is, a document guaranteeing that the customer's bank will pay you on set terms and conditions— say, when goods are supplied or when they are dispatched. A letter of credit is more commonly used in overseas transactions. Probably more widely known is the bank guarantee. Small business people are often required to give their bankers personal guarantees. Why not get bank guarantees from your customers to ensure that they will pay you? Subscribe to the trade journals to keep an eye on bad debtors. Watch the economy and think about the industry you are in and the industries that your customers are in, and whether there are any adverse economic conditions that might affect their ability to pay.

Another form of protection against nonpayment is trade indemnity insurance, whereby you pay a fee to have your insurance company pay up if your customer doesn't pay. Legal action might be considered as a last resort, but weigh the costs involved and remember that there is still no guarantee that you will get paid.

Trusting relationships with your customers is probably the most efficient way of guaranteeing payment. Should they get into financial trouble, they're sure to pay you first if you are a friend, the one who sees them socially.

Building Good Relationships

In the context of increasingly impersonal business practice, you are more likely to receive positive attention and to be successful (and not only in the area of debt collection) if you can build amicable and trusting relationships with the key players in your particular field.

Most people realize the importance of getting on well with their customers. But don't forget your suppliers. If you have always paid your creditors on time, then they will allow you extra credit should the need arise, and this might be particularly valuable in tough times. Don't abuse your creditors. Develop a good rapport with them, be honest with them, and be worthy of their trust. Get close to them. Perhaps take them to the theater or to something else of mutual interest. Treat your creditors fairly and warmly, and, should things go badly for you, they may treat you fairly and warmly in return. They will think of you in personal, rather than statistical, terms.

The same applies to your banker. The biggest problem for bankers is that small business people don't talk to them enough. Don't hide from your banker; face up to and confront the issues that concern him or her. Provide your banker with a business plan (see Chapter 3). Update him or her with financial statements every month, every six months, or every twelve months. Tell him or her of your cash flow requirements.

Attend to your budget and liquidity problems. Let your banker know in advance if you need any extra money or, especially, if you have any extra money to invest. Get close to him or her. Get advice. Your banker is very experienced; he or she has a lot of small business clients and might well pass on valuable information to you. When you need that extra credit, your banker will allow you to have it, provided he or she knows you will pay it back.

Don't make promises you can't keep. There's nothing worse for a lender or a creditor. If you say you will pay by the fourteenth of the following month, make sure you do pay by that date, if not earlier. Don't keep making excuses. If you make a commitment, be sure to stick to it. Bear in mind that bankers are highly trained and highly audited. Their files are detailed. They are avid writers; they record every conversation and keep very detailed file notes. You should do the same. If you make notes and record your conversations with the bank, you will be in a better position to stand by the agreed-upon arrangements.

Your accountant, like your banker, should be someone you talk to regularly. Develop a friendship, get free advice, invite your accountant home to dinner, and let him or her contribute to your business plan. Get your accountant involved in your business, but not too closely. (Accountants have to remain impartial and professional so as not to lose their independence.)

Underlying your relationships with your accountant, your banker, and your creditors are the needs for communication, honesty, and trust. These needs are as important to business as any other factors. Everyone wants to deal with someone who is honest and trustworthy because there are so many who aren't. If you are honest and upright, you may offer a service or product that costs more, and you may not be able to deliver it as quickly as someone else, but because you are a friend, because you are trusted and liked, you will clinch the deal and get the order. Suppliers will supply you before they supply someone else because they want you to be successful. Your customers will pay you on time. Your banker will give you that extra advice. Your accountant will return your call and give you those extra few minutes or that extra bit of devoted energy that is necessary to help your business survive and achieve its profit and goals.

6

MANAGING A SMALL BUSINESS

Managing a small business is very similar to managing your personal affairs. You must make sure that you budget properly and that more money comes in than goes out. There are perhaps a few more complications when it comes to business, but people who can manage their personal finances tend to be able to manage their business finances as well. This chapter offers detailed suggestions for the effective management of a small business.

Getting Good Advice

Many small business operators make the mistake of trying to do everything themselves. They would never contemplate doing their own mail deliveries, yet they don't consult the experts in truly specialized areas.

For general advice, especially on finance, government small business agencies can be very helpful. In addition, build around you a team of useful advisers, each with his or her own field of expertise. Choose them carefully and don't base your decision on convenience, friendship, or family. The various associations and institutes will give you lists of members in your locality. Don't rush into a quick decision. Shop around, talk to a few people, have a few meetings. Find advisers who show empathy and care, can be trusted, are prepared to understand the needs of your business and are experienced. Don't be afraid of changing later if you are dissatisfied, just as you would if you were dissatisfied with your doctor. Good advisers bring objectivity to your business, possibly recognizing early warning signs that you may miss because you are too involved, and seeing problems for what they really are. They will put you back in touch with the wider economic context at the times when a fresh and ruthless perspective matters most.

Accountants

The first adviser a small business needs is an *accountant*. A good accountant can provide advice and assistance in all aspects of financial management, sources of financing, and application for financing. It is a mistake to use accountants only to prepare annual accounts and tax returns. Their expertise extends much more widely than this, and it pays to tap it. You should choose your accountant in the early stages of your business, when you are developing your plan, and periodically review his or her ability to service your business needs.

Make sure your accountant is strong and commands your respect. There's no point paying for advice and not taking it, which occurs too often. A good accountant can help an average business succeed, but an average accountant can help a good business fail. Deal with accountants who are successful themselves. If they can't manage their own affairs, how are they going to manage yours? Interview at least three candidates. Find out about their services and charges, and how they operate.

Choose an accountant who knows your industry and business area, someone who can readily determine from your monthly figures any potential financial problems or, especially, any potential opportunities. He or she will understand your business plan, your costs, and everything else that is peculiar to your business area. He or she knows who the lenders are and who the bad customers are. Good accountants are specialists just like other professionals. It's no good going to one who specializes in hotels if you are running a farm; each of these types of business requires vastly different knowledge and experience.

Talk to your industry peers. Ask them who they use, with whom they are satisfied, and who does the best job for them. Don't be afraid to use the same accountant.

You must feel comfortable with your accountant. It is no good going to an accountant who hasn't got time for you and doesn't answer your phone calls. Once you have found a suitable accountant, don't assume that the level of service is guaranteed. Rarely does the accountant who originally suited your business continue to do so throughout all its phases. The probability is that you will outgrow your accountant or your accountant will outgrow you. But, as mentioned earlier, a good personal rapport can help stem this process and hold your accountant's interest. If you get along well, you are less likely to be overlooked when your accountant is under pressure.

Most small business people start off with either production or sales skills and generally lack financial management skills. Therefore, an accountant is probably the most important adviser and is central to the business's financial management. So stay close to him or her; keep him or her involved and informed. Take your accountant to the first meeting with your banker. Consider inviting your accountant to your monthly or regularly scheduled meetings. Make sure you send the agenda for reading beforehand so that every second spent in the meeting is fully productive. Watch your accountant's charge-out rates. Make sure you get quotes in advance. Watch out for those accountants who charge you for the time you spend with them at lunches. (It's a good way for them to make money while they're being fed.) In hard times, when your business may not be doing too well, the choice of an expert accountant to come in and review your affairs might mean the difference between surviving and collapsing.

Bankers

Another important adviser is your *banker*. You should talk to your banker when your business venture is merely a glint in your eye. Tell him or her you are tossing around ideas and would welcome another opinion, even though you may not yet have identified your financing needs. A good relationship is important because your banker's experience enables him or her to provide worthwhile advice. If the bank is unable to accommodate your financial requirements, your banker can probably suggest the best alternative. Remember, banks deal with small businesses every day of the week. Among their many clients are those who have been around for a long time and have extensive experience. During the early stages of developing your business plan, your banker can often help by pointing out the pitfalls. Banks see the good and the bad sides of business; they know what it is like for families to be kicked out of their homes; they know what it is like to repossess. It is in their interests to try to help you not become a bankruptcy statistic.

Lawyers

Another important adviser is your *lawyer*. Proper legal advice in business may save you thousands of dollars and even a spell in jail. But seeking advice in a hurry may land you in trouble, so it is a good idea to start looking for a suitable lawyer before you need one.

The law is very complex, and legal practices tend to specialize in particular aspects of the law—for example, tax, contracts, tenancy, product liability, employee legislation and litigation, conveyancing, and so on. Make sure you find a lawyer who suits your needs in each particular situation. (This means you may end up using several, on different occasions.) Whether to use a large or a small firm very much depends on the size of your business. Initially, you might start off with a smaller firm, the bigger ones tending to be far too expensive and appropriate only for specialist advice.

Get referrals from friends and advice from your employer association as to who is the best in a particular area. There are lawyers who specialize in different industries. Try out one or two and make sure you find the right balance of trust, empathy, care, and professionalism. Legal fees can be costly, so make sure you get quotations before you engage the services of a lawyer.

Any legal agreement your business has or is considering should be examined by your lawyer to ensure your best interests are being protected. It makes sense to seek his or her advice on your options before decisions are made.

Case Study. Julia inherited a great deal of money due to the tragically premature death of her husband. At the age of thirty-two she had a house worth $320,000 without any mortgage, a $1 million life insurance payout, and a marketing/public relations/advertising firm about which she knew nothing. She had shared with her husband the responsibility of looking after their three children. What was Julia to do now?

Through her husband she had met a man who had been in the same business but was now retired. She knew he wouldn't be trying to compete with or destroy her business, so she trusted him. He urged her to get good advisers and, after much research, she ended up with a number of accountants and lawyers to choose from. She asked all the accountants who their existing clients were, where their money was invested, what business interests they had that might conflict with hers, how many employees they had, how much time they had available, how their health was, and whether or not they would be accessible to her. All three accountants sounded impressive, but only one took the time to present a detailed analysis of Julia's personal and business financial position. He got a new client.

As for a lawyer, that choice was slightly more difficult. Eventually Julia chose one who had the toughness to compensate for her lack of confidence, who knew the industry and was able to advise Julia on the legal aspects of continuing with the business.

The children are not seeing as much of their mom as they once did, but the business certainly continues to prosper.

Insurance Brokers

Insurance is of critical importance to small business. All lending institutions will insist that applicants for financing have sufficient insurance to replace stock, plant, and buildings, and to cover loss of profits. *Insurance brokers* should, therefore, be included on your team of advisers. Remember that in life you generally get what you pay for, and the cheapest may not be the best for you. Your broker will tell you what should be covered and by whom. He or she will get several quotes and choose the most suitable package.

Consultants

Another form of advice can be sought from *management consultants*, who usually specialize in a particular area, such as sales, marketing, finance, or production. Be very wary of management consultants. Work only with those who have proven to be successful in the past. Many consult because they lack practical expertise themselves. Make sure you get quotes from management consultants and any other consultants you engage, so that you know exactly what to expect.

From time to time it is a good idea to get a *sales professional* to come in and provide some inspirational sparks to enhance the performance of your staff. They can often set new standards and working styles. But make sure you tailor their input to your needs. Don't give them vague instructions—give them specific tasks and direction.

Stockbrokers and *investment banks* should also be mentioned, although they confine their advisory services almost exclusively to large companies. In special circumstances they may assist small businesses. For example, if a company has a sound and profitable venture in mind but few resources, an investment banker may be able to link up the company with potential investors. Alternatively, the bank may involve itself directly. Investment banks are generally willing to take comparatively high risks if the potential rewards are also high. In addition, both stockbrokers and investment bankers provide special advice and assistance on mergers and takeovers, and the latter may be willing to provide financial assistance.

Mentors

And finally, when selecting your advisers, don't overlook a *mentor* and/or an *external director*. In past societies the mentor relationship was commonly that between grandfather and grandson who lived in the same town or even the same house. The carpenter passed on his carpentry skills, the builder his building skills, the banker his banking skills, and so on. That social structure is now lost forever, but the benefits of the general principle still apply. A mentor, by definition, should be much more experienced, wiser, and probably older than you. Ideally he or she should have business expertise in the area in which you work, but a background in banking or finance would also be valuable. Listen to everything your mentor has to say and take his or her advice. At first it might make little sense, but in the long run you will be the better for having heard it.

A strong, experienced external director like the mentor can be invaluable to a growing business. Choose someone you trust and respect, someone to keep you in check and to guide, console, and encourage you when things are tough.

Networking

The exchange of useful information by people in a particular industry is known as networking. Networking vehicles can be formal, such as those provided by employer groups, clubs, societies, and courses; or informal, such as those that spring up socially, for example at the local gym. Whatever their context they are potentially very powerful in establishing and raising standards and in introducing participants to knowledge and opportunities.

Many self-employed business people are isolated by their need to work long hours and concentrate on the task at hand. This makes some form of organized interaction with industry peers even more important. You should take every opportunity to meet with other small business owners, talk to them, and listen to them. Much of the knowledge that contributes to running a prosperous business cannot be gained through formal training—it is gleaned through experience and passed on by sharing that experience. You will find that your peers also have cash flow, staff, and financial problems. They are probably going through the same things as you are. Listen to how they solve their problems and discuss your solutions with them. By talking to others in the same boat you can share ideas and concerns, be comforted, and help each other. It might be a good idea to organize a monthly breakfast with a group of like-minded business people.

The External Environment

You cannot afford to ignore the external economic environment in the running of your business. In fact, you should plan your business according to what you think the economy is going to do. You need only scan the business section of newspapers and business magazines to realize the extent to which our personal lives, let alone our business lives, are affected by oil prices, interest rates, politics, or even an apparently harmless statement by a politician.

The size of the impact depends on the specific industry and market you are in. For example, a rise in petroleum prices will have a greater impact on a transport company than on a company that develops computer software. A rise in interest rates will affect the demand for property and, therefore, decrease business prospects for real estate firms and property developers.

Increased demands on your work schedule in a tough economic climate are no excuse not to keep yourself informed. In fact, such a climate makes it all the more important for you to remain alert to the macroeconomic environment—to watch for external guidance, warnings, and opportunities. If you stick your head in the sand and focus only on the immediate problems of your own operation, you will lose sight of the big picture, the scene that really matters. Your business is only a cog in a big commercial machine—don't lose sight of its context. Read, listen, watch, and learn. Make sure you educate yourself in the meaning of terms such as *elasticity/inelasticity of prices, inflation, recession, depression, balance of payments,* and *tariffs.* Buy and borrow books, attend courses, go to your employer association meetings, and be part of a network of business acquaintances.

Whenever you hear or see a piece of economic, political, or even social or scientific news, always try to visualize how that fragment of information will affect your business and what impact it will have on your sales, expenses, customers, and suppliers. For example, if you are a retailer in a suburban shopping center and you learn by mail or by reading the local newspaper that there are going to be substantial street improvements going on for the next four months, what should you do? You don't complain—ultimately the improvements will benefit your business. You find out the exact details. Attend local council meetings; speak to the council's engineering department; and find out when the works are starting, what is involved, and when they will be completed. (Add on two or three months to allow for delays.) In anticipation of fewer customers, plan to reduce stock, to organize holidays for yourself and your staff, and to refurbish your shop. In other words, minimize your costs, budget for a reduction in cash flow, and take advantage of the opportunity. You will probably also need to pump up your marketing in order to warn customers beforehand and bring them back once the work is completed.

Familiarize yourself with trends and cycles, and take advantage of these in your business. You can even prosper from the hard economic environment itself. In a recession, people may do more work around the house. They cook a few more meals at home. They do more of their own car and house repairs because having less paid work gives them more time for unpaid work (for which they would normally have to pay someone else). They replant the garden because they can't afford to go away on holidays. In such times, the products that sell well are staples such as food, renovating materials, paint, garden accessories, plants, and housewares such as pots and pans—but only for the domestic market, not for the trade. Also, people cut back on big things (such as cars) and splurge on little things (such as clothing accessories and cheap entertainment) to make themselves feel good. Service industries that do well are those that clean up the mess—financial advisers, insolvency accountants and lawyers, and even antique and art auctioneers.

> **Case Study.** Carol was an enterprising retailer who, right in the midst of the recession, opened up a gift shop with a fairy theme. "There is nothing in the shop that anyone needs," she was quoted as saying. "I'm selling dreams, magic, and good feelings." At first she was afraid to tell her accountant about her undertaking, but within weeks of opening she was taking on extra staff and had been approached by two people wanting to franchise the business. Such was the misjudged pessimism of her suppliers that the only difficulty she experienced was keeping up with demand.

By the same token, businesses that might flourish in a recession need to watch for other external factors that might affect them adversely. Plant nurseries, for example, would be wise to take conservative action in the face of climatic disasters, such as drought or floods. The insolvency accountancy firm would benefit in better times from also specializing in, say, tax planning.

Furthermore, no two recessions are exactly the same, and their causes partly determine their effects on business.

You need to understand how all these factors might affect you. In your time management, be sure you allocate quality, concentrated time to absorb and analyze what is going on around you. Don't cling rigidly to preconceived ideas about your business or the context in which it operates. Be adaptable and innovative. (Remember the proverb: Necessity is the mother of invention.) Think laterally; allow your instincts to guide you; listen to other points of view. In tough times, when your head is down and your back is up against the wall just to keep your cash flow going, the assistance of your mentor or external director may be invaluable. Even though mentors may be under financial pressures themselves, they are still likely to bring a wider, independent perspective to your business.

Business Hardware

In your business plan, it is important to list all the physical needs of your business and to decide what you can afford and when.

Your business premises are one of your most important tools of trade, and there are many variables to consider. Should you work from home or from an office? How much space do you need? Should you rent or buy?

Make sure you locate well. Many small businesses fail to appreciate how costly bad positioning can be. Are you physically accessible to your customers? Are you in the ideal situation to receive and deliver goods to service them? What transportation is available for your staff? What other facilities are available? Will the staff be happy there? Is it safe and secure? Is theft a problem? Is there a risk of fire? Will you be proud to welcome your customers and visitors? What is the best way to get raw materials in and products and services out? It's in your best interest to ensure that your premises are safe; after all, accidents are costly.

If you are in the retail trade, how large should the store be? What merchandise needs to be displayed? Can more stock be securely stored? Are existing displays and shelving adequate for merchandising needs? Are counters and tools well positioned? Are there sufficient points of sale? Does the store layout induce customers to buy more? Are stock control methods adequate?

Vehicles are also important business hardware, and again there are many options. Should you use your own vehicles, or should you use leased or rented vehicles or courier services? What type of vehicles do you need? Do you need the headache of initially running your own vehicle and driver? Talk to your accountant about this. Make sure whatever you use has a profit or net profit result or net cash flow gain first and a tax benefit last.

Be careful when buying second-hand equipment—it can often cause problems. Frustrating delays or additional footwork through lack of forethought can adversely affect your workers and profits. If your machinery is delicate, regular maintenance is essential. The more complex the plant, the more thought you should put into selecting and acquiring your equipment.

Keep abreast of the latest technology and the equipment being used by your competitors. Business might be lost overnight to someone else who can provide a more rapid turnover or higher quality article at the same unit cost. Computers and their cost-saving advantages must be considered.

Find out about, and adhere to, government standards affecting production layout, storage of raw materials and finished goods, work safety, and comfort. Be one step ahead of the health and safety inspector.

People

It is no coincidence that labor costs eat up a large proportion of turnover in most businesses. Because quality of staff is the most important factor in any business of more than one person, you should always employ the best people you can obtain and afford. Friendly, skillful, conscientious employees will enhance work pace by putting in the extra effort—without complaint. If your employees are satisfied and feel cared for, they will stay put, and stable personnel will mean a more efficient business.

One of the great satisfactions in running your own business comes from building a solid team of workers around you who support and carry out the policies and plans of the business. But harmonious working relationships, high morale, and effective teamwork—features of the ideal staff—do not just happen. Bear these features in mind when hiring and foster them regularly.

Each person on the staff has a responsibility to all other members to perform his or her task efficiently and cheerfully, to help others willingly when their work requires it, to accept the authority that goes with the job, and to back up superiors loyally during the good and the bad times. In small businesses in particular, if there is just one person in the group who falls short in any of these respects, the efficiency of the whole team is reduced, not only in terms of total output but also in terms of influence on other members of the group.

Leading

The business owner has a particularly important role to play in the group by virtue of his or her position. As the leader, he or she must ensure that all members of the group get maximum satisfaction from their work, enjoy happy relations with their coworkers, and work with enthusiasm and efficiency to achieve the objectives of the business.

When you are employing people, make sure that there is a clear mutual understanding of the basis upon which they are being employed. If a new recruit is not a member of a union, you should provide a letter of employment that spells out the basis on which he or she is being employed, the pay, hours of work and duties, and what period of notice is required if either party wants to bring the situation to an end. This will save problems later on.

Staff members should have clearly defined jobs and the employer must see that they do them well. They should be given adequate initial training and then be allowed to work with just enough supervision to ensure that they keep up to the required standard. Constant close supervision is likely to lower a person's self-esteem. On the other hand, insufficient supervision allows errors to go uncorrected and makes workers feel that their superior is not interested in whether the work is done well or poorly. Staff members should know what is expected of them in terms of extent and the quality of work. If they exceed expectations, they are entitled to, and should receive, fair praise for their achievements. Recognition of one's efforts is always pleasurable, particularly if it has been genuinely earned. Empty praise is worthless.

If a person falls short of the standard, the wise employer does not just condemn without trial. Talk with the employee and try to find out the cause of the failure. The fault may be not with the person but in the work system—the tools, the conditions—or from lack of guidance at the outset or personal troubles at home. If you have been successful in building up a sound relationship of mutual confidence and respect, the worker will be glad to get such troubles off his or her chest and ask for assistance in putting things right. Be constructive in your criticism, and when mistakes are discovered, ensure that they are not repeated. Progress is not made without occasional errors, but you as the employer are failing somewhere if the same error occurs frequently.

Encourage your staff to learn new work so that they are gradually being prepared for more responsibility and greater rewards. Dull, routine jobs will be more interesting if the persons doing them not only understand the next step but are given some training in it. They also take a greater interest and more pride in their jobs if they are given some responsibility for training their successors.

It is important to keep your staff informed of your business objectives, so they can be motivated to the same extent to which you are, especially when the operation is small and growing. They must have the same or nearly the same amount of interest in, and understanding of, how the business succeeds—through selling, making a profit, and collecting the money. (Your business plan will serve to demonstrate this to them.)

If you can make the objectives of the employee and the objectives of the company one and the same, you have a greater chance of succeeding at both.

Delegating

Because you will often be unavailable, it is important to delegate authority and foster initiative, not forgetting that authority and responsibility go together. The ability to think for oneself and make decisions varies from person to person. The wise owner encourages staff members to work out solutions to their own problems, because decisions should be made as closely as possible to the level at which they are put into effect. Of course you should check each decision, but the people involved should be encouraged to suggest their own solution first.

Make sure all employees are doing the jobs for which they are best suited and that they don't have some undiscovered talents. Watch out for signs that employees are outgrowing their jobs and promote them at the right time. It may be hard to lose the services of a good worker to another area, but it is even harder to lose that worker altogether. More difficult to deal with are those who have come as far as their capabilities allow, but think they should be promoted by virtue of long and competent service. The best course of action here is frankness. Ask them if they really think they are capable of taking on higher positions. If they are sensible and the positions are clearly portrayed, they will probably admit that the work would be beyond them. While they will be disappointed, at least they will know where they stand.

Retaining

It is important to try to make the workplace as comfortable, practical, and enjoyable as possible, but not at the expense of efficiency. Make sure you get along with all your employees without becoming too close, and show them that you care about them. That is what really helps them to be motivated and profitable for you. Take an interest in their development. Care about their safety, health, and general well-being. Treat people as people, not as numbers on a payroll. Make it your business to know about any major personal problems and provide constructive help without becoming too involved. You should remain alert to any tension or uneasiness in, or among, your staff. You should watch for any lack of commitment or prevalence of a nine-to-five mentality, both of which denote staff discontent and undermine the prosperity of the business.

It is not always the big pay increase that will retain and protect your people. More effective are your appreciation and recognition of their efforts and achievements. Give them a "pat on the back" with flowers, tickets, gifts, lunches, or dinners. Fringe benefits need not cost a lot, but they may be just what you need to motivate your staff and retain them.

Of particular relevance in hard times is the skillful handling of grievances. Complaints should be examined clinically and without prejudice or blame to establish whether the underlying cause is a shortcoming of the worker or a problem with the environment, relationships with others, or the company's policies. Listen patiently with an open mind and distinguish facts from opinions. Get to the bottom of the real issues: Check the facts and consult with those involved. Be fair, be strict, but be careful not to set negative precedents. Exercise self-control, because emotions can run high in such situations. Resolve the issue by consensus if possible, but avoid unnecessary delays in reaching a decision. Discontent soon spreads, and speedy rough justice without prejudice or bitterness is far better than excessive deliberation over a decision. Explain your decision in a clear, straightforward manner and make sure you keep detailed records of all meetings and significant documents.

Make every effort to ensure that the work situation is safe and healthy. Safety is everyone's responsibility. You must not only provide a safe environment, but also ensure that employees take reasonable care. Adequate safety equipment should be supplied to each employee. Ensure that your business complies with relevant safety requirements. Provide safety training at regular intervals and perform safety audits at set times. Federal and state safety officials can assist in drawing up a safety policy and carrying out safety awareness programs.

In tough times there is a lot of pressure on the staff of a small business. Creditors phone frequently for payment and debtors aren't paying. More than ever in this environment, you need to communicate and be honest with your staff. Tell them your plans, expectations, problems, and opportunities. Carry out staff suggestions on ways to improve the organization. Set realistic targets and constantly review their work. If you are in desperate straits, you needn't reveal every last detail, but you should at least let your staff know what the general financial situation is. In hard times employees often start to worry about the viability of their employer, so it is far better to be honest about it than to have them inflate it and resign due to uncertainty.

Recruiting and Training

When times are tough, it is more critical than ever for you to select only high-quality employees. So a short note on recruitment methods is warranted here. Recruitment is a process of obtaining personnel who meet the requirements of your business. Although recruitment is generally applied to obtaining applicants from outside the company, many companies have an unrecognized source of applicants from within their own ranks. The possibility of transferring and promoting existing people should always be considered before taking on anyone from outside. Promotion from within can minimize the cost of training new people because the person concerned already has a knowledge of the company and its products. Familiarity with the company's procedures also makes adjustment to the new position easier.

Above all you should prepare a detailed job description. Of course it might change with time and as times get tougher, but it should be regularly updated. The job description should spell out the required job experience, skills, or education and training, as well as any other relevant requirements. Make sure that all information is detailed and accurate. Too often applicants are sought to fill positions to which little thought has been given. As a result, the wrong candidate is selected.

There are various ways of obtaining new staff from the outside. You can advertise in the papers and you can go through employment agencies. (These charge quite a substantial percentage of the first year's wages in fees.) You can advertise in industry magazines—for example, accounting magazines if you are looking for an accountant. You can also ask your existing employees and friends whether they know of anyone who is suitable for the job. (Be careful with this approach, though, and don't neglect your usual criteria for suitability.) Government agencies provide employment services that are appropriate in some circumstances.

It is a good idea to have all applicants write letters of application. This will reveal a lot about their language abilities, personalities, tidiness, accuracy, and so forth. Then go through the letters and divide them into three piles: one for interviews, one for doubtful applications that you will hold, and one for those who are clearly unsuitable. The interviewing process is very difficult. If you are like most small business operators who don't have the luxury of employing a specialized personnel manager, it is highly likely that you will have to do it yourself.

The selection process must measure three main things. First, it must measure the person's ability to do the job and how much training and supervision will be needed to achieve optimum performance. Second, given that duties and responsibilities change, especially in the areas of technology and economics, it must measure the applicant's experience and potential to learn new skills, to adapt to new methods, and to accept additional responsibilities, rather than relying solely on training and background. Third, in order to permit detailed person-power planning and executive development, the selection process must measure a person's potential for advancement within the organization and determine the special training he or she will need to be fully equipped for advancement.

Develop detailed questions to elicit this information and keep a checklist to remind you of them. Allow enough time for the meeting and ensure that there is privacy. Determine what other techniques you are going to use. It may be a good idea to develop an application form that could encompass some of the questions just mentioned.

It is important, then, to take time in the induction and training of new employees. Time you spend with them when they first come to you, teaching them about the business and letting them read the relevant parts of the business plan, could be invaluable in the future. While they are fresh they may have better ideas or new perspectives, so you should encourage them to talk freely to you and make constructive suggestions, even at this early stage.

Once you have recruited staff it is important to train them. Lack of training is the Achilles' heel of a small business. The real problem is not the availability of training courses, but getting the small business community to recognize the benefits of such training. For attitudes to change, the importance of training must first be recognized in the schools. For example, all newcomers should be taught how their employers' businesses stay afloat. Training is a big investment, so make sure you gain an adequate return on it. Before you send any of your staff on a training course, find out what the course is designed to teach them and accept that on their return they may suggest ideas for change. Employees should be encouraged to pass on what they have learned. It is good management practice to evaluate any completed training.

Letting Employees Go

If your recruitment procedure fails in some way, or if an employee's circumstances change and he or she decides to leave your company, you should have what is known as an "exit interview." The interview can be quite revealing about your own business. Ask why the employee is leaving and what could have been improved in the business to make the employee's job more enjoyable or make him or her more efficient.

Of course you have the right to do so, but it is not wise to suddenly fire someone in anger. It is much smarter to plan ahead. If you are contemplating dismissing an employee due to inefficiency or wrongdoing, such as suspected theft, hold at least two meetings and document them. (Ideally you should both sign the document as a true record of the discussion.) In the first meeting, give the employee one month to resolve the problem, otherwise he or she will have to go. Have the employee set certain objectives that you will then review. If the objectives haven't been met, the inefficiencies haven't been eliminated, or the errors still occur, then hold and document a second meeting (and a third, if it becomes necessary to dismiss the employee). Remember that the employee has every right to legal means to determine whether wrongful dismissal has occurred and perhaps whether he or she should be reemployed or paid compensation.

If you have given adequate warning, preferably in writing, stating the problems and the action required by the employee, then you are on fairly safe ground. Be honest about it, document the process, give warnings, and give the employee the chance to perform. If the employee doesn't perform after the chance is given, then dismiss him or her. There is no point in being a hero and trying to keep your people for humanity's sake or just because you are afraid of the possible complications of letting someone go. It is better to act sharply and quickly to reduce overhead so that your business can survive and pay the remaining employees.

Keeping the Books

Inexperience and incompetence go hand in hand to produce much small business failure, mainly through management's inability to generate sales, limit expenses, collect debts, and control investments in stock. These problems are often compounded by a lack of administration skills—the straightforward ability to record and account for the daily, weekly, and monthly transactions of the business.

Bookkeeping is often considered time consuming and tedious, but this is only true if a backlog is allowed to occur. When you decide to go into business, open up a business bank account and keep it separate from your personal accounts. This will facilitate clear record keeping.

Good accounting habits do not protect a business against failure; however, they are an essential first step in helping to avoid some of the managerial problems that lead to collapse. More importantly, the information made available to small business owners by sound accounting records allows them to assess personal performance more competently, to apply for supplier credit and bank loans, and to prepare tax returns. It also serves as a basis for future planning and helps to protect business assets from carelessness, errors, and fraud.

Some form of record keeping is essential for all business operations. The extent, nature, and detail of records maintained will depend on the type of business information required and should be subject to advice from your accountant (who might also be involved in setting up the records). Whatever records you keep, they must be meaningful and understandable. Unless you constantly refer to them, discuss what they show you, and act on the conclusions you draw from them, they are useless.

Every system begins with two types of information: receipts (money received from business activities) and payments (money spent in running the business). These are recorded in the form of primary records. Deposit slips record money deposited in the bank, and check stubs record most payments made. When payments are made in cash, a cash sales slip or receipt should be provided by the entity making the sale; this becomes the primary record. It is from these records that entries are made to the receipts and payments journals, so it is essential that they are complete. Receipts should identify these items:

- Name of the customer
- Reason for receiving payment
- Amount received
- Date of receipt

Check stubs should identify these items:

- Date payment is made
- Name of the entity to which payment is being made
- Reason for making the payment
- Amount paid

Additional records recommended for efficient bookkeeping include the following:

- Documents of various types
- Cash journal
- Bank reconciliation
- Production record
- Payroll record
- Sales record
- Petty cash record
- Fixed asset record
- Accounting records, as well as cash flow books, invoice books and wages books

1. Documents

The first accounting habit to develop is to support every transaction with a written record, however informal. These might include sales slips and receipts, cash register tapes, delivery notices and invoices, check stubs, and employee time sheets. These are the source documents that may be demanded by auditors, customers, suppliers, and tax investigators as proof of transactions.

Procedures should be set up for storing and processing the documents that you will receive from other organizations, such as invoices from suppliers. These procedures need not be complicated. In fact, the simpler the procedure, the greater the chance that it will be used consistently. By establishing and adhering to simple procedures for handling business documents, the small business owner will find it easier to collect customer debts, pay suppliers, and control levels of cash liquidity. The storage of source documents is also a matter that should be carefully considered and discussed with your accountant. Depending on your budget, the documents can be stored in anything from shoe boxes to elaborate commercial filing systems, on anything from loose sheets of paper to microfiche. Stationery stores supply a variety of storage files and filing cabinets at reasonable prices, all of which are suitable for storing documents. Whatever means you select, it should be logical, easy to operate, and protected from damage and misuse.

Here are some of the basic routines that should be considered when you are setting up the accounting framework for a small business.

- A system for recording and reconciling cash received and sales for the day
- Procedures to ensure that credit is extended only to authorized customers and within their agreed credit limits
- Procedures to ensure customers are billed correctly and promptly for the goods they have received on credit
- Procedures for receiving goods (Delivery notes or packing slips should be checked against goods when delivered.)
- A system of payment for goods and services (Do invoices agree with delivery notices? Are prices correct? Is the arithmetic correct? Even computer-generated accounts can be wrong, as can bank statements.)
- Procedures for ensuring that staff members are paid correctly (This will involve checking time sheets, pay rates, tax installments, and so on.)
- Procedures to ensure that the inventory records correlate with the physical stock on hand

The effectiveness of these procedures will be enhanced by segregating, wherever possible, the duties performed by employees of the business. For example, the employee who receives cash should not be responsible for reconciling it or banking it. The employee who receives incoming goods should not perform the inventory reconciliation alone or be responsible for payment of suppliers. In a small business it is not always possible to segregate all the duties, but you should seek to allocate tasks as sensibly as you can.

Many people are unfamiliar with the paperwork of business; many are uncertain of the relationship between delivery notes, invoices, and statements; and many find it confusing to determine exactly how much they should pay for goods and services rendered. Generally, a packing slip is intended as a memorandum of goods received; an invoice is a detailed list of amounts charged for each item received and a record of accounts payable to the supplier; and the statement records the balance due, made up of the current invoices payable plus any balance payable from the previous months since the last statement was issued.

Learning how to match packing slips with invoices and invoices with statements is not difficult. Advantages to be gained include reducing the probability of under- or overpayment of accounts, allowing your business to gain valuable purchase discounts where available, and protecting the business's credit reputation. Source documents such as these are evidence of transactions. Transactions must be recorded if they are to provide the information for the purposes that are intended, such as measuring performance and adhering to the business plan.

2. Cash Journals

Well-kept cash records are essential for keeping track of the business cash resources. They also mean that your accountant can prepare reports and returns more quickly. Provided there is a concise record of all receipts and payments for any period, they eliminate the need for the accountant to analyze check stubs and receipt books—a time-consuming and error-prone task. They also provide a convenient breakdown of the various kinds of receipts and payments.

When you are starting off in business you should do your own manual cash journals and records. This is the only way you will know exactly how much money you are spending. It is one thing to write out checks from time to time, but another to sit down, add them all up, and reconcile them. Balancing your own accounts allows you to get the totals that show what is physically going out and what is physically coming in, and to compare the two—money in versus money out.

Normally these cash records will have a date column; a column showing who the payment is to or from; a reference column that gives the source document—either a check stub or a receipt book number; the amount column that should tally with the bank's; and various other headings that make sense to the business. A good accounting habit is to record receipts and payments from their source documents into journals at regular intervals, say daily or weekly. If performed regularly, the task is not unpleasant and allows you to make a regular check of the business's cash position.

The accuracy of the journals can be checked in two ways. First, the total of all the breakdown columns should equal the total of the amount column. If there is any disagreement, check both to see that they have been completed properly. Second, a bank reconciliation should be completed each month on receipt of the bank statement, or more frequently if your cash flow requires, even daily or weekly. This provides a valuable check on the accuracy and completeness of the amounts shown in the journals as well as information on the state of the business's cash resources. It will also reveal any errors made by the bank.

There are various ways to record cash journals, computers being one way of hastening the process. But the business owner should still be involved personally. The design of the journals will be determined by the kinds of transactions about which the business owner requires individual information. For instance, one owner may need to know the amount spent on gas and oil as a separate amount from what is spent on auto repairs. Hence, his or her financial report should show two separate amounts relating to motor vehicles. If these are regular kinds of expenses it makes sense to design a cash journal that includes a column for gas and oil and a column for auto repairs. You should discuss in detail with your accountant those transactions that are to be collected and reported as individual amounts. From these discussions the accountant will probably draw up a chart of recommended headings for the different divisions.

3. Bank Reconciliation

Many small businesses leave this in the hands of their accountants, but there are real advantages in you doing it yourself at least monthly or more often. By maintaining cash journals like those discussed, it is very easy for you to do your own bank reconciliations.

The business's cash balance in its own records is the difference between the total of its cash receipts and the total of its cash payments. If cash receipts are greater than cash payments, the cash balance is positive. If payments exceed receipts your business is in trouble, unless you have an overdraft arrangement with the bank. The balance of the cash account is determined by taking the previous balance and adding to it the total receipts for the period as per the cash receipt journal, and then subtracting the total cash payments for the period as per the cash payment journal.

Sometimes this will vary because there will be a time lag between checks being sent out and being presented at the bank. Therefore, adjustments have to be made. Also, deposits listed in the cash book may not necessarily appear on the bank statements yet. Again adjustments have to be made. Third, charges levied by the bank and sometimes periodical payments that you have authorized for, say, leasing must also be noted in the cash journals. You need to reconcile what is shown in your cash books and what is shown in the bank statements.

It is also important to check your figures in your cash book against the bank statement figures to ensure that the amounts have been recorded accurately in the cash book and that checks have been written accurately. Similarly, for the cash receipts, you have to make sure the bank deposit slips are accurately recorded in the cash receipts journal. Checking off each receipt or payment in the cash book as it is listed on the bank statement is a simple matter, as is determining outstanding deposits and checks and making sure that the bank has not made any mistakes. (Banks are certainly not infallible. In one instance, more than $100,000 worth of checks had gone into the account of someone else with the same surname and first initial!)

In summary, the steps for reconciling a bank statement are as follows:

- Review the bank statements for fees, charges, and periodical payments; adjust the cash books as necessary.
- Compare the bank deposits with the receipts in the cash receipt book and increase the bank statement balance by the total of the outstanding deposits.
- Compare the checks paid by the bank with those listed in the cash payments book and decrease the

adjusted bank statement balance by the total of the outstanding checks.

- Determine the balance of the cash account according to the cash books and make changes if necessary.

4. Production Records

For manufacturing businesses, production records aid in job costing. They allow the business proprietor to determine the labor and material costs of products and to compare them with expectations. When adequately designed and well kept, these records are an important source of information for the business.

5. Payroll Records

The sole proprietor has a legal obligation to the tax authorities to maintain adequate payroll records. Payroll records provide a basis for meeting legal obligations. Furthermore, the employer is required to issue statements to employees each year showing the amount of tax that has been deducted from their salaries. Payroll records allow this to be performed accurately and promptly.

6. Sales Records

Some businesses may find it impossible to assess performance and plan future operations without keeping a record of sales figures for different areas.

7. Petty Cash Records

It is usual to keep a small amount of cash on hand for the payment of petty or minor expenses, such as stamps, newspapers, coffee, tea, and so on. Such money should not be taken from the cash register. It should be kept separately and recorded and balanced daily or weekly. The use of "IOU" vouchers should be discouraged.

8. Fixed Asset Record

A fixed asset record is often required by an accountant for vehicles and other office equipment and property. Usually the accountant will require from the client the cost of any fixed assets purchased during the period, the amounts received for any assets sold during the period, as well as the date when such purchases or sales occurred. This also applies to other asset records, such as shares and investments that may be held in the business name.

9. Accounting Records

From the accounting records of the business the accountant will produce financial reports (see "Putting It All on Paper," in this chapter). Sadly, the only use made of these reports by many business owners is for the preparation of company tax returns. Yet, as stated earlier, they provide important data for assessing the performance of the business in order to plan future operations and to identify any problems, especially when generated more than once a year.

Here are other important records.

- Accounts receivable (debts), which records who owes you money, how old the debt is, and how much is owed. (A simple card system will do, summarized on a page with lists of customers who owe you money and amounts divided into days or months outstanding.)

- An inventory or stock record. (Again, a card system will suffice if computers are not cost effective.)

- Accounts payable (credits). A well-organized set of paid and unpaid accounts from creditors is often sufficient for business to control payment of their accounts; however, a card or equivalent system may also be used and summarized on one piece of paper, listing all the creditors, ages of the outstanding amounts, and total amount.

Costing and Pricing

There's no point in making a sale unless you profit and collect. Costing and pricing are very important in this equation.

Too many people in business don't know what their activities are costing them. They manufacture something and they sell it, yet they don't even add up the costs of the materials they used to make it. Even if they do include materials, they forget their own labor. Or, if they remember materials and labor, they undervalue them. They also forget about rent, overhead, wages, and state and federal taxes. They forget to include the interest on borrowed money. When it comes to calculating their selling price, they are motivated only by making a sale.

Costing, more than anything else, seems to frighten off people in small businesses. Most are more interested in the production of their article than in the correct costing of it. While many successful entrepreneurs rely on their noses to arrive at a selling price, today's fierce competition and high costs underline the necessity of ensuring that each item is properly priced. Inflation also plays a role here. Today's products must be priced to allow for today's expenses. Therefore, some basic knowledge of costing is essential. To maximize profit the owner must understand the different types of costs and how they behave.

So, what does your product/service cost? There are three aspects to this. The real costs to any business are first, its labor cost, particularly your own; secondly, the cost of external borrowing; and finally, other fixed and variable costs.

Take the following steps to calculate an hourly labor rate.

STEP 1 Calculate the total actual cost of labor

Gross wage of employee @ $320 per week	$16,640 per year
ADD cost of benefits, holidays, vacation, unemployment, and worker's compensation at 17.5%	$2,912
Total actual labor cost	$18,496

STEP 2 Calculate the total hours available

Available time = 5 days per week x 52 weeks	260 days
LESS vacation @ 4 weeks per year	20 days
LESS sick days @ 5 days per year	5 days
LESS public holidays @ 10 days per year	10 days
LESS long service leave @ approximately 5 days per year	5 days
Total days available	220 days

STEP 3 Calculate total productive hours per year by multiplying daily productive hours (assuming an 8-hour day with one unproductive hour) by total days available

$$7 \text{ hours} \times 220 \text{ days} = 1{,}540 \text{ hours per year}$$

STEP 4 Calculate cost of labor by dividing total actual cost by total productive hours per year

$$\frac{\$18{,}496}{1{,}540} = 12$$

STEP 5 Calculate the overhead rate per direct labor hour by dividing estimated manufacturing overhead by estimated direct labor hours

For the purposes of this illustration assume $6 per hour.

STEP 6 Calculate the labor rate by adding the result of Step 4 to the result of Step 5

$$\$12 + \$6 = \$18$$

STEP 7 Calculate the mark-up on the labor rate as shown in Step 6 (Assume 25% mark-up)

$$25\% \text{ of } \$18 = \$4.50$$

STEP 8 Calculate the charge-out rate by adding markup to labor rate:

$$\$4.50 + \$18 = \$22.50$$

Even if you do not have staff, you still have labor costs—your own. In calculating what you are worth to your business, consider what you would be paid for doing this sort of work elsewhere. Don't forget to allow for annual leave, that is, four weeks' wages plus 17.5 percent loading, or the equivalent in overtime.

The second aspect of costing is the cost of external borrowing (that is, interest and fees) and any dividends to be paid to external investors. The most common form of external borrowing for businesses is a line of credit. The cost can fairly readily be determined by looking at the charges that come through monthly or quarterly on your bank statements. Also in this category are the interest costs on personal loans, fully drawn advances, mortgages, and so on. With the help of your accountant, you should be able to calculate the cost of these loans, as well as any other costs and interest charges in rental and leasing arrangements.

Finally, assess your fixed costs and variable costs and how they affect your profit margin. Fixed costs are the costs of staying in business and do not vary with sales levels. They include rent, insurance, telephone, possibly other expenses, and also leasing charges for all capital equipment used in the business. Variable costs are the costs that vary with turnover or production. The most important of these is the cost of raw materials (or of goods sold, in retailing) and the labor content of the business where it is directly related to production or sales. The less important variable costs may be auto expenses, power, and so on.

It is the balance between fixed and variable costs that makes for the profitability of the business. These factors are used to calculate the break-even point, or the level of output at which total sales equals total costs of the business. The break-even point can readily be calculated by dividing fixed costs by the so-called "contribution" (sales revenue minus variable costs) per unit. The result indicates how many items must be sold to make neither a profit nor a loss for a particular year. The break-even point can be lowered by decreasing fixed costs, decreasing variable costs, increasing selling prices, or a combination of all three. It is very useful for planning purposes.

Break-even is absolutely critical, no matter how small or large your business is. Obviously the bigger the business, the more sophisticated the system needed to calculate it. In a small business you should know, on a day-by-day basis, exactly how many sales are required to make a profit. You should know what your overhead and fixed costs are, on which day of the week you have made a profit or a loss, on which day you have broken even, and when you will start to make a profit. Do you have sufficient sales by Thursday so that Friday and Saturday mornings, if you are in a retail business, are profitable? There is no business that cannot be broken down on a weekly or daily basis. If you cannot do this then you haven't done your costing and calculated your break-even properly. And if you don't make the profits you should make, you are probably going to go broke.

A number of factors govern the appropriate pricing of goods or services, but basically prices must cover all costs, both variable (those that change with numbers sold) and fixed (those that don't change, regardless of turnover). There must be a return to the owner that reflects the risk, effort, and money invested. Other factors to be considered include the following:

- Pricing policies of competitors.
- Price sensitivity of the product or service. (Will higher prices result in customers switching to other suppliers?)
- Price consciousness of customers. (Is the target market more interested in price or quality?)
- Level of overhead costs to be covered.

Specials—offering certain products or services at low prices—can be used to induce customers to visit the business. Cutting prices is often advisable for slow-moving or redundant stock or services.

Selling on credit can often increase sales and might be necessary for expensive items, for businesses dependent upon cyclical income received by their customers (for example, country stores dependent on the custom of farmers), or for businesses whose customers need to make regular (say, monthly) purchases (for example, pharmacists).

What is the best selling price? In setting prices the goal must simply be to maximize profits, not to maximize sales. Although some business operators feel that increased sales volume is needed for increased profit, volume alone does not mean more profit. Profit is made up of three ingredients: cost, selling price, and the unit sales volume. The desired profit is achieved by adjusting the respective proportions of these. No one pricing formula will produce a greater profit under all conditions. Up-to-date knowledge of market conditions is also necessary because the "right" selling price for a product under one set of market conditions may be the wrong price at other times. The best selling price for a product is not necessarily the price that will sell the most units, nor is it always the price that will bring in the greatest number of sale dollars. Rather, the best price is the one that will maximize the profit of the company. The best selling price should be cost-orientated and market-orientated. It should be high enough to cover your costs and make a profit for you. It should be low enough to attract customers and build sales volume.

The most common form of pricing by small business owners is markup pricing, as distinct from demand pricing. This system uses the cost of the product or service as a base and then adds a markup, usually a percentage, to this base. Mark-up is not the same as gross profit margin. Gross profit margin is always less than the markup. However, it is extremely important for a small business to know and understand the concept of gross profit margin (and how it differs from mark-up), because it is this proportional percentage of each dollar from sales that is used to pay overhead, wages, and taxes, to establish reserves, and to provide a return to the owner. To calculate the gross profit margin all you need to know is the percentage markup.

Pricing really comes back to what the market will bear. Often you are better off to charge a higher price. For example, if you quote $1,200 instead of $1,000, and if your customers feel they are getting good value, then you would have been foolish to quote the lower price, even though the item only cost you half of that. If competition occurs or other factors come into play, you can always bring the price down. I know this notion may be hard to grasp, but you should never undercharge. You should, if anything, overcharge.

Case Study. Ted was a lawyer who studied accounting as Paul's student before practicing law. He started small, in a smart office in the city with one staff member and a huge library. Paul wanted to set up his own company trust but, in those early days, didn't know much about how it was done. Paul went to Ted out of loyalty. Even though it was only his first year in business, Ted charged Paul twice as much as anyone else would have. What's more, before Paul even had a chance to complain, Ted was taking steps to collect his money.

Today Ted is a lecturer in Law, has successfully floated two public companies, is an expert adviser on the board of several major legal firms, and works about a quarter of the hours Paul does. I guess Ted had it right from day one. He believes in his product and he believes in himself. He's charged the maximum and he's collected his money.

It is worth reiterating here the importance of the opportunity cost, or the value of your own money. If that money were not tied up in the business, you could be investing it and earning 10, 12, or 15 percent (the going market rate), or you could be putting it into property and earning something that way. Consider what effect it would have on the net profit of the business if you charged, say, 12.5 percent for the use of money you have invested in the business. Is there any compensating growth in the goodwill of the business so that if you sold out you would realize a capital gain? Look at the net profit of the business before taking account of your own labor and the effect of charging interest on your own money invested. Then deduct these expenses to arrive at an adjusted net profit figure. Are you left with any profit? If you are left with the figure you expected, you must weigh the nonfinancial advantage of continuing and then decide whether your business makes adequate use of your labor and the money you have invested.

Case Study. Stuart had a small automotive repair shop with lots of sophisticated equipment. He had an established client base, but he never made any money. He was working formidable hours, usually starting at 6 A.M. and not finishing until 10 P.M. He worked six and a half days a week. The rest of the time he worried about the business and wondered why he wasn't making any money.

A quick analysis of his business showed some major strengths—established client base, good location, good equipment (if anything, too much), and only one weakness: too much stock tying up his cash flow. It appeared that he was barely charging out his own labor and just covering the cost of his materials. He wasn't keeping accurate wage records and had no labor time records at all.

He was advised to increase his prices. The thought was inconceivable to him because the business had been his father's for many years and he didn't want to upset anybody. Eventually, after many discussions and the recalculation of his costs, he was talked into increasing his prices—by 200 percent!

He kept his materials at cost, with a small markup for packaging and travel, and charged correctly for labor. To his amazement, the only customers he lost were bad payers anyway, so he was better off without them. His profits increased dramatically; he had more time to spend at home with his six kids; he could have the vacation he had always looked forward to; and he could assist his parents, who weren't very well off. He was a new person.

Often in hard times small businesses see a reduction in sales without a change in margins. How do you cope with this? Well, you have to try to reduce your fixed costs by reevaluating your product and services and perhaps discarding unprofitable lines. Guard against assuming that a particular line cannot be cut out. Call in somebody else (your mentor or an accountant) to analyze the situation objectively; you might be surprised to see that the bottom line return comes from another line altogether.

Increase your margin if products or services are not price sensitive. Consider decreasing your direct cost by obtaining greater discounts or substituting cheaper material stocks. You should also reduce your stock levels to cope with the cost pressures and reduction in sales.

Any decrease in sales will cause a loss in revenue that will also decrease your working capital. One way to cope with decreasing sales is to decrease your prices and run sales on slow-moving stock. Reassess and reduce your borrowing to reduce interest paid on borrowed funds. Check cost efficiencies, especially fixed costs, to offset squeezed profit margins. Reassess capacity needs and, if necessary, dispose of surplus assets, equipment, staff, and stock. The best strategy for increasing profits is to increase volume, improve profitability, and reduce expenses.

Budgeting

It is very important in business to know where you are going and how to get there, in other words, to make a forecast in the form of a budget.

Budgets have many uses. They assist in communicating to you, your banker, and key personnel the cost and overall charges involved in your planned operation. The budgeting process provides a bench mark against which actual performance can be measured, thus serving to motivate, set targets, and encourage the delegation of responsibility. Budgeting can be used for forecasting, for planning, and for controlling. Depending on the type and size of the operation, some or all of the following may be necessary: a sales budget, a production budget, a profit and loss statement, and the all-important cash budget.

Budgets, though, must not be rigid. They must be flexible enough to accommodate not only controllable costs but also those beyond control. They must also allow for sales or production fluctuations.

Part of the budgeting process is to determine the break-even point. Break-even is the point at which sales volume, in numbers and dollars, covers the fixed expenses of the business and you start to make a profit. Profits result from selling goods and services at a price high enough to enable the business to pay all expenses, including the cost of goods sold, and to have a surplus remaining. The break-even chart is often a useful tool to combine with your budget, as it reveals useful ratios.

It is important to complete the budget before the financial year begins, even though the actual results of the previous year will not be known in precise detail. If this is not done, the discipline of performance measurement will lapse in the first month of the year. If the monthly reporting procedure is in operation (in "Putting It All on Paper," in this chapter), the production of annual accounts should not reveal any surprises.

The budget should be prepared and constantly reviewed by those responsible for achieving it because the past is often the best guide to the future. In practice, the budgeting process will normally start with last year's achievement. The figures will then be adjusted to reflect planned changes. Even in a stable business, adjustments will have to be made for inflation, expected wage settlements, and changing interest rates. The main weakness of this approach is perpetuating the mistakes of the past. For an expanding business these mistakes can be multiplied. It is a good idea to attempt to prepare budgets from square one. This technique is known as zero-based budgeting. It is a useful device for examining the business objectively and questioning established procedures. If you have ambitious expansion plans, zero-based budgets may be the best alternative.

Despite the critical importance of sales turnover, many small businesses find it impossible to estimate and therefore have trouble preparing accurate budgets. This difficulty can be overcome with flexible budgeting, or the process of estimating sales turnover at various levels and preparing for it.

Cash Flow Budget—International Products Inc.

Sales	July	Aug.	Sept.	Oct.	Nov.	Dec.	Jan.
Processing	3500	3800	4000	4000	3900	3400	3500
Photography	2000	2800	3000	3000	2200	1000	1500
Printer	8000	10000	15000	15000	12000	6000	7000
Graphics	64500	89900	129000	126000	103400	53600	59500
Film	2000	3500	4000	5000	4500	1000	1500
Other	10000	20000	25000	27000	24000	5000	7000
Total Sales	90000	130000	180000	180000	150000	70000	80000
Less Cost of Goods Sold							
Opening Stock							
Subcontractors							
Purchases	22500	32500	45000	45000	37500	17500	20000
Photography							
Processing							
Other							
Work in Progress Movement							
Cost of Goods Sold (25%)	22500	32500	45000	45000	37500	17500	20000
Gross Profit	67500	97500	135000	135000	112500	52500	60000
Selling Expenses							
Advertising & Promotion	1000	4000	4000	2000	1000	500	500
Entertainment	40	40	40	40	40	40	40
Exhibitions/Trade Fairs				6000			
Travel/Acc./Overseas	310	310	310	310	310	310	310
Brochures/Printing	3000			2000			
Administration & General							
Audit & Accounting				1259			
Legal Expenses							500
Power—Light				1000			
Cleaning	20	20	20	20	20	20	20
Insurance			2700			1500	
Motor Vehicle Exps.	1800	1800	1800	2000	1800	1800	1800
Insurance—Workcare	1301.4	1440	1440	1440	1440	1440	1476
Long Service Leave	143	143	143	143	143	143	150
Service Contracts	3000	3000	3000	3000	3000	3000	3000
Rates							
Repairs & Maintenance				1000		1000	2000
Salaries & Wages	14460	16000	16000	16000	16000	16000	16400
Staff Amenities	50	50	50	50	50	50	50
Telephone	1000	850	2000	1000	1200	500	2000
Rent Paid	1921	1921	1921	1921	1921	1921	1921
Superannuation	500	500	500	500	500	500	500
Financial Expenses							
Bad & Doubtful Debts							
Bank Charges & Interest	300	300	300	300	300	300	300
Debt Collection Exp.							
Interest—Other &							
Lease Payments	12176	12176	12176	12176	12176	12176	12176
Loan Repayment					20000	20000	20000
Total Expenses	41021.4	42550	46400	52159	59900	61200	63143
Net Cash Position	26478.6	54950	88600	82841	52600	-8700	-3143
Cumulative	26478.6	81428.6	170028.6	252869.6	305469.6	296769.6	293626.6

Feb.	Mar.	Apr.	May	June	Total	Year Two	Year Three
3700	4000	4000	3900	3700	45400	68033	88443
2000	3000	2500	2450	2000	27450	41000	53320
9000	15000	13000	13000	11000	134000	200843	261100
87300	129000	112750	115150	99800	1169900	1754850	2281300
3000	4000	3750	3500	3500	39250	58900	76600
15000	25000	24000	22000	20000	224000	336374	437237
120000	180000	160000	160000	140000	1640000	2460000	31980000
30000	45000	40000	40000	35000	410000	615000	799500
					0		
30000	45000	40000	40000	35000	410000	615000	799500
90000	135000	120000	120000	105000	1230000	1845000	2398500
1000	4000	3000	2000	500	23500	7000	8000
40	40	40	40	40	480	550	640
		7000			13000	18000	24000
			18000		18000	22000	26000
310	310	310	310	310	3720	4600	4800
	2000				7000	10000	12000
1250					2509	2759.9	3035.89
					500	550	605
		1000			2000	2200	2420
20	20	20	20	20	240	360	400
		1000			5200	5720	6292
1800	1800	1800	2000	1800	22000	26000	35000
1476	1674	1674	1674	1674	18149.4	19964.34	21960.77
150	150	150	150	150	1758	1933.8	2127.18
3000	3000	3000	3000	3000	36000	39600	43560
			1375		1375	1512.5	1663.75
	500			1000	5500	6050	6655
16400	18600	18600	18600	18600	201660	221826	244008.6
50	50	50	50	50	600	660	726
10000	1500	2000	1000	15000	38050	41855	46040.5
1921	1921	1921	1921	1921	23052	25357.2	27892.92
500	500	500	500	500	6000	6600	7260
					0		
300	300	300	300	300	3600	4400	4600
					0		
					0		
12176	12176	12176	12176	12176	146112	75000	15000
50000	40000	50000	50000	50000	300000	364200	
100393	88541	105916	111741	107041	880005.4	908698.7	544687.6
-10393	46459	14084	8259	-2041	349994.6	936301.2	1853812
283233.6	329692.6	343776.6	352035.6	349994.6			

It is important that estimates be verified from time to time, certainly more regularly than annually. Many poor estimates will become apparent from reviewing the management reports themselves, while others will be corrected the following month when facts are known.

By comparing the monthly results with the budget, you are appraising your performance in implementing the plans. Do not waste time explaining any small difference that arises each month. Trends, however, must be observed and explanations obtained for continuing variations. Remember, the purpose of comparison is not to amuse your accountant, but to enable management to identify action required to maintain or improve business performance. This is why you need management reporting systems. If they do not assist the decision making process, the system or the management must be changed.

Obviously, if variations occur, such as an unusually large expense item, greater control and pruning are required. But even an increase in sales over budget may not be in the best interests of the business if it is due to a windfall that will not be repeated, while in fact traditional sales have severely declined. Therefore, your budgets (and financial reports) need to be detailed enough to detect any unusual occurrences so that immediate corrective action can be taken.

Budgeting provides a realistic estimate of income and costs for a given period and the financial situation at the end of that period. The budget should be designed to do the following:

- Enable the result of your business operations to be measured. (Separate budgets will probably be needed for sales, production costs, and overhead.)
- Show sufficient details to allow significant variation from budget to be identified.

- Avoid any confusion regarding responsibility for each section of the budget.
- Meet the profit targets determined.
- Be compatible with your reporting systems, so that you understand it sufficiently to act in a timely fashion.

Budgets are the basis on which to make sound business decisions as changes occur and on which to make comparisons between budget and actual results. By analysis of the result you can pinpoint where the estimates went wrong and can make decisions and enact strategies to correct the problems and/or capitalize on opportunities. Budgets provide a basis on which to make day-to-day decisions during the set period, and a guide to management for setting reasonable targets and objectives.

Cash Flow—The Lifeblood

Cash flow is the lifeblood of any business, and like the blood in your veins it must be kept in circulation. If you are cut, and blood flows out and cannot be stemmed, you will eventually die. It is the same in a business. If costs go uncontrolled, if you don't move the cash around, the business dies—it is as simple as that. Cash is the main element of working capital, and it is management's job to ensure that the business trades within its cash cycle. The cause of many insolvencies can be traced to poor understanding of the need for adequate cash to pay the bills.

Today, most lenders realize that the key to successful financing and lending is accurate and tight cash flow. They usually look for evidence of this in realistic forecasts prepared by prudent and careful business owners showing precise management of stock, debts, and credits.

In times of inflation, availability of financing is restricted by the overall increased demand and restrictions on credit. At the same time, interest rates are higher; this further compounds the problem. Inflation boosts the extra cash required by businesses due to the need to replace stock that costs more than the original stock. Many expenses run high, and there is a push-pull effect of creditors seeking earlier settlement in contrast to debtors wishing to settle much later. The result, of course, is a reduction in cash in hand. This forces up borrowing and further rations the capital required for expansion. If this is not available from external sources, the company reserves are diminished.

A common failing among small business people, particularly in contracting or in businesses where payment is received up front, is the belief that cash in hand equates profit. When cash is freely available, they go out and spend it on peripheral items, nonessentials. On the day of reckoning, they are in all sorts of trouble. You must manage cash prudently and estimate in advance how much cash is required. This can be achieved through the cash flow budget forecast. When a surplus occurs, it can be invested to earn interest for future needs. When shortages are anticipated, you have sufficient advance notice to plan and investigate borrowing and its alternatives. Hard-core expenses can be planned, particularly those of a capital nature or involving an increase in stock. Rapidly rising cost trends can be observed and spending planned accordingly. Policy related to extent and timing of purchases and terms related to credit given and credit anticipated can also be carefully considered.

Cars, plant, and equipment are among the major capital expenditure items for small businesses. Typical mistakes in this area are the purchasing of a plant with excessive capacity; purchasing too many assets; premature acquisition of land and buildings; purchasing equipment that commits the business to out-of-date, unsuitable, or uneconomical methods of production; or purchasing equipment because it is tax deductible. Will the machine itself or the articles it produces become obsolete in the short term? What finance is required to purchase the asset? The decision on capital expenditure must be very carefully considered in the business plan.

Another potential drain on cash flow is the holding of too much stock. Many people starting out in business are seduced by the persuasive powers of sales people offering discounts and bulk purchase deals. But remember, stock is unrealized sales; it is cash sitting on the shelves or in the warehouse. As the saying goes, "If it doesn't sell, it is very expensive." That is the reason why people go broke—they have too much stock or the wrong sort of stock.

Imagine your stock to be twenty-dollar bills. How carefully would you look at it then? If you fail to control your stock in the long run, it will be dollars that you will be losing. Stock control simply involves being aware, by whatever method you find most convenient, of the level and condition at any time of anything purchased or manufactured by your business. This control should start much earlier than most businesses realize, and should not finish until the goods have finally been converted into hard cash. Simple forms of control can be devised according to the needs of the business. Stock cards will normally suffice. Minimum and maximum levels should be set, as well as quantity to be reordered when the lower level is reached. These figures will naturally depend on usage, as well as the time it takes to obtain new supplies. A careful balance is needed between the danger of running short and the expense of overstocking.

Money tied up in stock is not working to the benefit of the business. Apart from the actual cost of buying required stock (whether raw materials or part-finished or completed goods), other expenses are involved. It is estimated that merely holding stock can cost up to 20 percent of its basic value. Other costs can include holding charges, interest costs, losses or damage, obsolescence, handling, paperwork, and so on. Nowadays, most multinational companies do not carry stock at all. They work on an automatic computer buying system to bring in their raw material stock from outside parties once an order has been received.

Stock turnover has a considerable effect on profitability, particularly in retailing, where a high proportion of funds are employed in financing stock. Stock turnover in these types of businesses is the hard core that truly spins the cash cycle. Gross profit margin dollars accumulate in direct proportion to how frequently the stock is being turned over or how hard this part of the working capital area is working.

Such is the critical importance of cash flow that many a small business operator spends more time fighting a rear-guard action with creditors than he or she does managing the business. This form of preoccupation is like a disease, but it need not be terminal.

As already noted, creditors are often one of the major sources of short-term funds for the smaller company. Although they appear as a liability in the financial statements, friendly creditors are a valuable asset, even when trading is normal. When times get tough and you need the additional finance or cash flow, a friendly creditor can allow you to extend your terms for payment and to survive.

Earlier in this book you saw what an important role the collection of debts plays in maintaining the cash flow of a business. Debt collection has a stronger-than-usual tendency to fail in hard times, with former thirty-day payers taking sixty or ninety days or longer because of their own cash-flow problems.

Another potential drain on cash flow is the proprietor who takes too much out for personal use. You may be tempted to reward yourself for all your hard work by taking an overseas trip or buying an expensive car. But a substantial proportion of the business's profits should be retained in the business for increased working capital needs—to finance equipment and the inevitable growth of stock and debts as your business expands—and, particularly in difficult times, to put away funds as a buffer. Remember, if the business is your main source of income, then you and your income are interdependent. You need to ensure the security and future of both.

When a business is short of cash it is *undercapitalized*. This means that the total funds available to run the business are inadequate for the efficient conduct of the business. If that is the case, the business becomes too dependent on its creditors. Undercapitalization or insufficient working capital leads to the following losses and inefficiencies.

- Missed opportunities to purchase materials offered at a favorable prices
- Need to get rid of stock at an unprofitable price simply to obtain badly needed cash
- Inability to afford sufficient materials to keep the production line running or to replace plant and equipment
- Constant distraction by day-to-day money problems, instead of focus on business operations (management by crisis, not management by objectives)

Businesses that are undercapitalized can run into difficulties from circumstances entirely out of the manager's control, as well as facing the problem of actually going broke due to an inability to pay current liabilities. The main thing is to keep your financial backers satisfied.

If, on the other hand, the business is overcapitalized, with more than sufficient funds to finance both its fixed and working capital, the question of what to do with the excess will arise. Surplus cash should be put to work immediately to generate additional funds. Before making investments that can tie up surplus cash for long periods, small business owners should set aside a cash reserve that can be withdrawn quickly to meet any unforeseen contingency. Interest-bearing deposits with banks and savings and loans are a popular parking spot for such reserves.

Control of payments is also of prime importance. They should be made on the due dates—not before and certainly not after. If clerical inefficiencies are causing loss of cash discounts on accounts payable, steps should be taken to eliminate these inefficiencies.

In summary, the small business person can optimize cash availability by accelerating collections, making payments on due dates, having few bank accounts, and studying cash flows, including the relationship between cash flow and bank balances. In hard economic times, when one needs to live with borrowing, the manager of any highly leveraged company must ensure that the cash flow provides for all maturing liabilities and the interest on borrowed funds. Above all, you must know your exact cash position (liquidity) at every moment of every day, particularly in hard times. You must know where your cash is and how much is available. You must know exactly what your bank balance is, based on the assumption that all checks issued have been cleared. A simple transaction book will serve to document this. Here are some additional ways to improve your cash flow.

- Use a credit card system for customer payments. It is better than the company carrying its own accounts receivable.

- Send out invoices as soon as the goods or services have been supplied. Set priorities for preparing invoices. If all invoices cannot be promptly mailed, try to process the biggest amounts first.

- Ask for up-front payment of part of the bill—in other words, a retainer. Some businesses are also in the position to bill on an interim basis.

- Charge interest on delinquent accounts.

- Convert to a "pay on invoice only" system; in other words, drop the habit of sending out monthly statements. It only costs money and allows the customer extra time to pay the debt.

- Arrange to send orders and invoices before the end of the month. An invoice dated June 30 will be paid earlier than one dated July 1.

- Sell on shorter terms (for example, payment required in 14 days rather than 30) and follow up earlier.

- Drop small customers who don't pay promptly. Focus on large customers who pay on time.

- Guard against selling to customers who are in financial difficulties. Be alert to any radical changes in buying or repayment behavior.

Finally, you should constantly be looking for better ways to borrow money or finance any current debt. Be ever vigilant. Superior cash flow management is clearly an essential art, for cash flow is a vital component of both corporate performance and its measurement—profit. For many, it is the critical factor.

Putting It All on Paper

Closely connected in importance to budgeting and cash flow forecasting is reporting for the business—recording its day-to-day activities. Reporting takes the stress and the chance out of running a business and replaces these with control. Your records should always be kept current; they can be rather tedious to update retrospectively.

Your accountant will advise you on the specific types of records you should keep, depending on the needs of your business. The main ones are the cash book, which records all cash entries, including checks and payments; the sales and purchases record, which records payment to creditors and sales to customers; a record of your assets; and other records. All these records are then used to prepare financial statements—or numerical representations of your efforts, your mistakes, your achievements—your blood, sweat, and tears.

No matter what financial statements a small business uses, the important thing is to understand them. You have already covered basic bookkeeping methods, but it is one thing to have the information at hand and another to be able to read it. It is no good having your accountant or bookkeeper prepare sophisticated profit and loss statements and balance sheets if you don't look at them or if you do look at them but don't understand them.

Apart from the cash flow statement, which was already mentioned, the two most common types of financial statement are the profit and loss statement and the balance sheet.

Profit and Loss Statement

The profit and loss statement for a business is the measure of its profitability. The income, or sales revenue, represents your market—what you have sold, how much you have sold, at what price. Expenses, which come next after sales, represent what you spent to earn those sales—that is, what money has been expended in the course of the period covered to immediately generate those sales. It does not include assets that are purchased and that will produce income in the future, such as plant and equipment. Here is the difference between expenses or payments that appear in a profit and loss statement and payments that appear in the balance sheet. By comparing apples with apples, you are comparing income generated in a particular period with expenses incurred and spent in earning that income.

Balance Sheet

The other document, the balance sheet, represents the actual net worth of the business, that is, what it is worth at a particular point in time. It is calculated by deducting liabilities from assets to arrive at the net worth of your equity (known as owner's equity, or sometimes called partnership's or shareholders' funds). The assets mentioned previously are assets that produce income. They can be plant and equipment, motor vehicles, land, or anything that produces income for more than the period over which the statements have been prepared. Liabilities, on the other hand, obviously represent money you owe to banks, creditors, finance companies, and so on.

By comparing the status of assets and liabilities from month to month you can determine the financial performance of your business. The profit and loss statement shows the short-term profit or loss for a given period. The balance sheet represents the result of those profits and losses accumulated over a number of short periods to show the net position or net worth of the business. The cash flow statement, the profit and loss statement, and the balance sheet,

Three Financial Statements

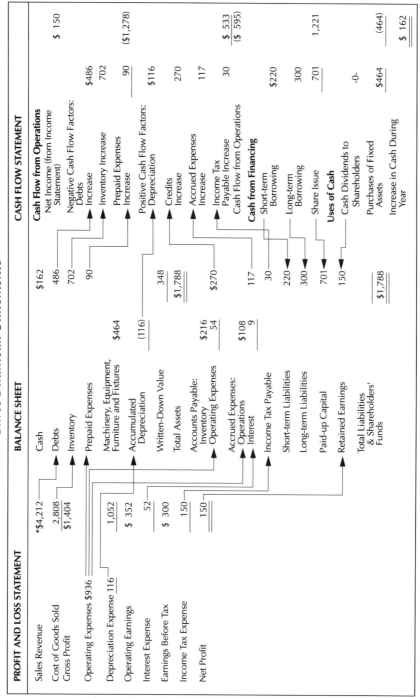

(*Dollar amounts in thousands)

when read in conjunction with each other, give a total picture of the financial status of your business.

The three financial statements shown on page 166 relate to the first year of trading of a small manufacturing business. The important connections are shown by arrows. Reading these connections is a little like looking at a chessboard in the middle of a game. Each piece must be studied in relation to the other pieces so that an overall pattern and situation can be understood. A detailed analysis of these relationships is given in the Appendix.

When it comes to reporting and bookkeeping, it is a good idea to do things manually first, before rushing off to use a computer, so that you develop a basic understanding of how book records are to be kept and financial statements drawn up. Just as you should initially do your own production, your own selling, your own debt collection, and so on, do your own bookkeeping under your accountant's guidance and you will get a feeling for how your business is going. Look at it on the paper in front of you; look at what you have actually spent versus what you have actually earned.

Don't get too sophisticated. Sometimes people who have orchards or neighborhood grocery stores have the best accounting systems of all. They know just how much things cost them each day. Grocers know exactly what their costs are at the market, exactly what they have to charge for apples and pears per pound to make a profit. They know that they have to sell things at a certain price to make a profit. They also know what their shop is costing them, how much rent they are paying, what their fixed costs are. They don't use computers, but they still make a profit.

One-Page Summary

A very important report for every small business owner is the one-page summary. This should be prepared at the end of every week or at least at the end of the month. It summarizes all the reports and relevant figures that have already been mentioned. The one-page summary sets out your financial position, your performance, in these terms.

- Sales for the period
- Purchases for the period
- Expenses for the period
- Net profit for the period
- Break-even point

It also gives a picture of your financial health—stock level and debts versus bank and other credits—to ascertain your liquidity level.

Make your one-page summary in your diary. You should look at it daily, compare it with last month or last year, and constantly pore over it to get an accurate picture of how you are doing. Here is a sample.

The One-Page Summary

Sales		Purchases	
Division	$		$
Division	$		
		Overhead Expenses	
		Selling	$
		Administration	$
		Finance	
		Interest	$
Subtotal	$_____	Subtotal	$_____
Net Profit (Loss)	$_____		
Assets		Liabilities	
Bank		Bank Overdraft	$
Debtors Total		Creditors Total	
30	$	30	$
60	$	60	$
>90	$	>90	$
Stock	$		
Subtotal	$_____	Subtotal	$_____
Net Working Capital	$_____		
Fixed Assets		Loans	
Plant	$	Leases	$
Land	$	Hire Purchase	
Subtotal	$_____	Subtotal	$_____
Net Worth	$_____		

This suggested format allows you to compare your weekly or monthly profits/loss performance. It enables you to compare your current assets with current liabilities to determine your cash liquidity position. It breaks down debts to see whether any problems exist in payment to you, and credits to show whether you are having any difficulties, and to what extent. It also reviews your long-term assets versus liabilities to arrive at your net financial position. The business operator who uses a one-page summary is almost always successful.

Meetings—Who Needs Them?

The typical entrepreneur often finds meetings a bore. But meetings are an inevitable and important part of business life, be they with bankers, creditors, customers, or your own directors, boards of management, and employees. Meetings are frequently held in restaurants. Meeting over a meal is better suited to small numbers (ideally two) and is friendlier and less formal. If you are the host, you will have the advantage that your guest(s) will usually be more vulnerable and receptive. However, these sorts of meetings are better for marketing than for matters requiring a less distracting environment.

Meetings should be held at a fixed time and with a strict agenda. Minutes of the previous meeting, even reports that are to be tabled, should have been circulated as early as possible before the meeting. Everybody should arrive on time and the meeting should begin as scheduled. The meeting shouldn't go on for hours because people's attention spans simply don't last that long. The meeting should begin with recording or reviewing the previous minutes and what action has been taken as a result.

Directors' meetings with your external director or mentor in attendance (and your accountant invited when appropriate) should be held monthly. The agenda suited to your business will follow the headings in your business plan and will address general matters, discussed in this book—cash flow, bureaucratic regulations, and so on.

Meetings to do with more detailed matters, such as marketing, staff, and business hardware, should be held weekly at a time and place that does not interfere with the running of the business, preferably early in the morning when everyone is fresh and eager to get to the point.

If meetings achieve their purposes, they are not boring and are certainly not a waste of time. Meetings are a forum for communication. They can be used for brainstorming and for creativity. It is a good idea to get away to a different place where the phone doesn't ring, thinking can take place freely, and discussion can occur. Meetings also can be a venue for solving interpersonal problems in the workplace. They give people the chance to discuss things honestly.

If you are just starting out, you need not have an elaborate board meeting, but you must sit down once a week with your mentor, spouse, or someone close to see how your week has gone, to analyze your sales and your costs. Remember to meet with your accountant once a month. Since this costs money, you must use the time effectively. Send your financial figures to him or her beforehand, listing what accounting services you require. If someone does your books for you, he or she should attend the meeting to help explain the figures.

If you have any doubts or there is something you don't understand, your mentor or external director should be available to answer your questions. That person might also help to make sure you are doing the right thing—not spending too much money, working hard enough, not feeling sorry for yourself. Unless you have inordinate powers of self-discipline, you will need someone there to keep pushing you—someone you respect and will take notice of. You can't always deal with yourself efficiently unless you refer your concerns and activities to someone else. It is almost like going to the teacher and reporting on what you have done for that week. It can be quite painful and annoying and seems like a waste of time, but it gives you the chance to look at yourself in a kind of mirror.

Time Management

The typical entrepreneur has too much to do and too little time to do it in. Most small business people work more than fifty hours a week, but without effective time management much of their activity may well be wasted, particularly when they are tired or under financial stress. They may be frittering away hours on trivial, insignificant, or irrelevant activities, while leaving vital tasks undone.

Two things—time and energy—are available to everyone, but they are not always used to the same effect. Your use of your energy and time determines how effective you are in business. Learn to control your business rather than letting it control you. It comes back to self-discipline.

Planning

The best way to find out how effectively you are using your time is simply to write down exactly what you are doing every fifteen minutes for a full twenty-four-hour period (allowing for sleep) over two weeks and reflect on it at the end of every day. You can go to as many time management classes and courses as you want to, but this is by far the most effective method of improving the use of your own time.

Effective managers put urgent jobs before less pressing ones, or first things first. They rank duties according to importance, deciding, for instance, which is more urgent—planning a new advertising campaign or hiring a new assistant. The best approach for tackling both routine duties and on-going projects is the preparation of daily, weekly, and monthly time management schedules.

You may want to plan for the week the Sunday before, going through your diary for each day. This process often reveals clashes. There are sometimes duplications of tasks and roles, and of meetings. You may find that rescheduling will in fact increase productivity, not only for yourself but for your staff as well. In your planning, you should allow time for emergencies and interruptions such as telephone calls. Depending on the sort of business you are in and how dependent you are on the telephone for communication, you might allocate times of the day when you make and receive all your telephone calls. Such systematic arrangement of tasks allows sufficient lead time for preparation of due-date material and all those disagreeable last-minute rushes.

Effective time management also means that your subordinates, particularly your secretary if you have one, can use their resources more efficiently. Lead from the front: If you are an inefficient user of time, your whole operation will tend to be inefficient.

Part of the process of managing your time is managing your mind. Very often, when you first start up a business your mind is highly active. It develops all sorts of ideas, envisages problems, and works out solutions. This can happen at eight o'clock at night or at three in the morning. To unburden your mind, you should write all these thoughts down. Your mind is a bit like a computer, in that it has a vast but limited capacity. Making a note of your thoughts is like freeing up the hard disk by copying data onto floppy disks: It creates space for more thinking. Don't worry about losing sleep; use the time wisely. If your mind wants to work let it work; if it doesn't want to work let it rest. Also, writing something down is a commitment. Once you have performed this physical act, you have provided the momentum for taking action. The agony of facing a task on the list and the ecstasy that comes from crossing it off when it is done will give you the incentive to repeat the process, so write everything down and make sure you act on it. Don't change priorities on your list and don't back out. If you have made a note to accomplish a task and you don't get to it, carry it forward to the next day in your diary.

Just as you plan for the full week on Sunday, organize for the next day at the end of the previous day. This will give you peace of mind at night, a feeling that you are on top of things, and a real excitement about going to work the next morning. Simply by arranging the next day, defining on paper what you want to accomplish, you will feel you have a head start. Meanwhile, your mind can begin working for you on the subconscious level. Also look back on the day just completed and review your accomplishments. List any matters that were not dealt with and must be carried forward.

There are four basic steps to planning a day.

1. Schedule time on your next day's page for appointments and meetings and consult your weekly and monthly calendar for details of what is ahead.

2. On a plain page, schedule time for sleep and other leisure activities (for example, family activities).

3. Work on your activities page: Assign priorities and schedule time on a planned page for, say, "A" activities or "B" activities. "A" might be for business activities, and you might set their priorities as 1A, 2A to 10A, or however many activities you have. "B" might be for leisure activities such as family, social, fitness, and hobbies.

4. Invest at least ten minutes at the end of each day to record your achievements, record your expenses, and plan for the next day.

Planning ahead can include not only the week, but months and years—indeed, five years as per the business plan. It is all part of using your time efficiently to achieve your business (and personal) objectives. It is mostly a matter of maintaining control of your business by forcing activities into the time available rather than trying to expand the time to accommodate the activities. Many people fear that if they don't seem out of control they are not going to seem busy enough or important enough. They really don't want to manage their time well. Once you realize that controlling your time is not only more productive but more pleasant, the rest is fairly easy.

Don't leave unfinished business or anything hanging over your head. Work intensely to create moments of empty space—a minute, an hour or a weekend— in which to enjoy having nothing to do. These moments are the carrots at the end of the stick, and by programming them into your schedule you force yourself to finish the business activities leading up to them within the times specifically allocated. Such valuable "free time" might allow for a problem to be solved or a new idea to arise.

An itinerary, a schedule, or a task allocation is worth-less unless you stick to it. A large part of sticking to your schedule is being aware that very few interruptions are so important that they have to be attended to immediately. Treat unexpected situations as you would any other time commitment. Don't respond immediately, but program time for dealing with them into your future schedule according to your priorities—that afternoon, tomorrow, or next week—whenever you can fit them in. Sticking to a schedule is also made easier by allocating the appropriate amount of time to the activities that will fill it up.

Don't try to do too much: You will end up frustrated by not doing anything properly.

Since most of the time in business you are dealing with people, you need to allow for personality. Everyone operates at a different pace. Some people are very quick on the telephone or in meetings and don't enter into much dialogue; others, by their very nature, like to talk at length about football, the weather, and so forth. Also, some people require more than one meeting, or protracted discussions and negotiations, to achieve objectives. Others, according to their personalities, circumstances, or places in the hierarchy, make decisions quickly. Try to learn as much as possible about the people you are dealing with, including employees. Get to understand their personalities and plan your time to accommodate them.

Often it is a good idea to do the things you least like doing at the beginning of the day to get them out of the way, or do quick tasks to build your sense of confidence and momentum for the rest of the day. Most small businesses have day-to-day problems of some sort (liquidity, dealing with banks, dealing with legal situations such as demand letters), especially in hard times. Ideally, you should allocate these to one or two times in the week, for an hour or so. This keeps the rest of the week free from thinking of, handling, or even accepting phone calls about such unpleasant, dreaded matters. It allows you to concentrate fully on the productive, profitable side of the business—your marketing, quality control, and cash flow. In your diary or the day's activity planner, schedule these a week in advance; then you won't neglect them and you will be more efficient in handling them. Equally importantly, you won't be tempted to set another priority ahead of them.

The best way to master time is to do the things you planned to do when you planned on doing them and within the time you allocated for them.

A useful aid to time management is a very efficient filing system, one that suits you. So much time can be wasted trying to find a letter, report, or note, not to mention personal paperwork, such as your will and all your household bills. Include in the filing system notes of all your conversations, no matter how brief, no matter how seemingly trivial. Learn by the example of your banker and lawyer. File all records of conversations under the client name or by subject, whichever makes more sense in your business. This will enable you to recall readily the conversation in the future, or to produce documentary evidence in the event of a dispute or an allegation. It could even mean the difference between losing or winning a court battle.

Delegating

A critical aspect of time management is delegation—the process of assigning appropriate chores to subordinates so that you are freed from routine operations. Failure or inability to delegate often entangles the small business owner in everyday activities at the expense of important ones such as planning, marketing, and collecting cash. Symptoms of failure to delegate are obvious: the small business owner who is too hurried to be effective, the owner who makes costly mistakes in dealing with customers and staff, or staff members who are unable to take over in emergencies when the boss is ill or absent.

Autocratic or perfectionist small business owners rationalize their reluctance to delegate by insisting that no one can do the work as well as they. Ask yourself whether this is really the case. Surely there are some tasks that can be delegated to subordinates or lower paid employees. Proper training is the obvious foil for this obstacle. Make certain your subordinates understand their responsibilities, the limits of their authority, and the results expected of them before they are turned loose on the task. Discuss their errors and show them ways of profiting from their mistakes.

Management experts stress one golden rule for successful delegation: Take on the jobs you dislike or are not familiar with and delegate the ones you know and love. Managers who perform favored tasks and pass on distasteful chores fail to acquire new knowledge that can help their companies' future profits and succeed in losing the esteem of their staff. If you find it simply impossible to delegate, for whatever personal reason, recognize this as a weakness and at least employ others who can do what you don't want to do yourself. This should form part of the strengths and weaknesses analysis you do right at the beginning, in your business plan.

The Burden of Bureaucracy

One of the major operating costs to business is government red tape. Form completion and compliance with a myriad of regulations place a heavy burden on the small business operator's time at the expense of productive business activity. The only way to cope with this is to be aware of the regulations and dutifully comply with them, even if you don't understand them or have scant regard for them. Consult your accountant if necessary.

Marketing

You saw earlier that the first ingredient for success is to make a sale. But sales don't happen automatically. You must find, woo, and win your market. This is hard enough in good times; but in tough times the entrepreneur has to work harder, smarter, and longer to achieve sales.

You may have objections at this point: "Marketing! We need to sell more products, earn more money, survive. The marketing's obvious." And so it may seem. But among the confusion and pressures of small business, particularly in hard times, it is vital to be disciplined and to know where you are going. A similar concept applies to the armed forces, where young recruits are drilled in polishing their boots and making their beds in a certain way. Why? Does this make them better fighters? The real point is discipline. If they perfect self-discipline they will study and train better and they will prepare their equipment more efficiently; therefore, making their beds and polishing their boots every morning will, indirectly, make them better fighters. Likewise, the marketing plan discussed in Chapter 3 is a form of discipline. It forces you to set schedules and expense budgets. It tells all those around you exactly what is required of them and when.

The rationale behind marketing is really very stark: No matter how brilliant your service or product, or how cost effective or cost saving you can be to others, the phone will not ring unless you tell people about it. Once they are aware, you must then ensure that you can satisfy their needs, profitably. Ways of alerting your potential clients to your product or service are many and spectacularly varied. They include print media, radio, television, brochures, direct mail, lecture circuits, personal selling, word-of-mouth support, social and club contacts, posters and signs, and so on. Publications exist that can guide you in choosing the most appropriate means for your business.

Using the Marketing Plan

Using the business plan outlined in Chapter 3, you will have established the marketing edge of your product or service and researched your competition. From the marketing plan built around that research you will have a clear picture of your objectives; where you are going to position your product; the target market you are after; your pricing and trading strategy; the logistics of delivery; your administrative support; your required sales force; the advertising, promotion, and public relations you are going to use; the resources you require; and finally your budgets and targets.

Strict adherence to sales budgets becomes even more important than usual in tough times, because sales will generate the profits that enable you to pay your overhead and your own wages. Sales budgets should clearly itemize each of the main costs, and where and when staff should be employed and trained. They should also break down your products and services into different segments.

If you have sales staff members, let them know what marketing you are undertaking and what expenditures you are incurring. Ask for their opinions and show real and obvious concern for them. They are far more important than a computer printout. Delegate to them as much responsibility as possible. Use the budget and sales forecast to deepen your understanding, not as an exercise in accounting practice. Make the budget interesting and easy to use. Change and redraft the whole budget if it proves to be wrong and limiting. A sales budget will be valuable only if it produces information that is relevant, timely, easy to assimilate, and easy to understand. It must be produced quickly, in time to be of the most use, with a high degree of detail, and as concisely as possible. Above all, it must be usable by the people who are to benefit from it.

Keep your plan tight and to the point. Short, sharp statements should be included. For example, a statement under your context heading might be like this: "Marketing objectives to ensure existing clients know that our company is the best in its field."

In hard times, concentrate on face-to-face marketing. Face your customers; go to their offices; see how they operate their factories; understand how they think. The best way you can market yourself to them, no matter what you are trying to sell, is to get to know them, make them your friends. One way to do this is to have a card on every customer, chief executive, or purchasing officer of the customer you are dealing with. Record personal details—quirks, interests, sports, musical tastes, and so on.

Understanding Customers

Also understand your customer's business so that you can offer alternatives that are acceptable. Understand your customer's seasonal peaks and valleys, stock, and stock control generally. Understand how customers earn their profits and assist you in trading term flexibility or otherwise. (Customers who earn cash—for example, fast-food outlets—should pay cash.) Generally, people like to know that someone cares about them, socially and professionally. It is nice to receive a birthday or anniversary card and congratulations when your particular team wins. You must service, service, and service your customers in every acceptable way imaginable, without going over the top. Don't rely on mail; the direct approach is preferable to the lazier third-party style, though it has a place in certain circumstances.

The cheapest marketing database is made up of leads and referrals from existing satisfied customers, not an expensive mailing list or advertising in glossy national magazines. It is one on one; it is being where your customer is. Find out through your own market research where your customers are and bump into them there. Be at the social occasions, get their business cards, and then choose how, when, and where you wish to contact them. If you are constantly found where your customers are, they will start to think, "Well, this person is doing all right because he or she is in my sphere of activity."

The formula for successful marketing is footwork, friendship, and trust. What do the insurance companies often do when people first join them? They get them to go and sell to all their friends and family. Just like your accountant and your banker, a customer faced with ten phone messages is obviously more likely to call you back first if you are a friend. This certainly makes life more enjoyable and has the added financial reward that your customers are going to prefer to deal with you, regardless of the comparative merits of your product or service.

One method of cutting back marketing costs is to target and direct-market your customers. This must then be followed up with written materials. Keep in constant contact with your customers. You will get the order if you are there at the time.

> **Case Study.** Allan is in the computer business and sells mainframe computers. He is dealing mainly with large corporations or government bureaucracies, and his orders range from $2,000 to $20 million. He will spend months and occasionally years just building up a relationship before the person has even identified the need to buy a computer. He is developing a relationship with a view to making a sale, and he usually reaches his target. In some cases, of course,

the company is taken over before he achieves his aim, but that is the risk he has to take.

The way in which your telephone is answered gives your customers a window onto your business. A bright, cheery, helpful receptionist will do more for your marketing than you will fully appreciate. You know that it makes you feel good to deal with a firm when you are on hold for only a short period of time and the receptionist keeps coming back to you. There is nothing worse than being on hold for an eternity and being assaulted with recorded music or an irritating radio station. The physical makeup of your reception area is also important, and you might like to adorn it with flowers, magazines, or even candy for your customers.

Don't overestimate the marketing potential of trade exhibitions or conventions. At a recent accounting convention, it was impossible not to notice the healthy supply of computer software, investment opportunities, and accounting services. But one very small booth that stood out even more was occupied by a company selling leather products—diaries and so on. It attracted the most interest. Perhaps the investment advisers and computer people would have been better off marketing their products at something totally unrelated, such as a food exhibition, where they would have been more noticeable.

If you decide to use advertising as one of your marketing tools, be sure to get a return on your advertising investment dollar. Use your dollar strategically and monitor and measure its effectiveness. There are no hard and fast rules as to how much you should spend. Each organization varies. Some allow a proportion of the sales that are expected to result.

But before contemplating advertising of any kind, establish who you are trying to attract and what you wish to achieve. Advertising starts at your front door. Carefully study your existing customers and try to introduce new products to them. Request introductions to other divisions and/or subsidiaries. Even try for introductions to your customers' customers. It is the most effective and most immediate placement of your advertising and marketing resources. Once these avenues have been exhausted, establish who you are going to attract to your company. Approach the market with a clear picture of what you hope to achieve.

> **Case Study.** Catherine has a hotel with the best restaurant in the area. She was always overbooked on Thursdays, Fridays, and Saturdays, but rarely had reservations on Mondays or Tuesdays. She began an advertising campaign aimed at the type of people who frequented her restaurant from Thursday to Saturday. She advertised in the print media and spent ten times her advertising budget with absolutely no sign of increased sales.
>
> Her mistake was that she didn't aim her advertising strategically. It was common sense that if existing customers rarely ate out on Mondays and Tuesdays why should similar types of customers from a wider area be any different? Realizing this, she decided to target a particular group and try to attract them by making a series of special offers. These included a free meal for any senior citizen having lunch with a paying customer. This was designed to entice the existing customers to bring their parents. Also, any group of six or more would get a 25 percent discount. Budget-conscious seniors started enjoying the restaurant on Mondays and Tuesdays almost immediately. Catherine also employed a day-care worker to assist parents with their children when they came to lunch or dinner on a Monday or Tuesday. The advertising was inexpensive and very effective. It consisted of a local suburban newspaper advertisement and notices sent to local clubs and day-care centers.

When it comes to selling, you can use what is the called the ABC customer selection process. The most profitable customers are classified under category A. They are serviced very efficiently and given the most attention. Customers in a sort of limbo, who will either blossom into category A or will eventually be placed in category C, are classified under category B, and are visited and supported slightly less than the A customers. The C-category customers may receive a visit or telephone call from the company once or twice a year, but their needs are serviced by sales staff who will explore opportunities or problems as they arise.

Maximizing Sales

If you employ sales staff, don't confuse the role of a sales professional with that of an order taker. The sales professional is distinguished by certain qualities, the first of which is courage. It certainly takes courage to earn one's income purely from commission or brokerage. Second, sales professionals must have detailed knowledge of their markets and of their customers. Third, they must be able to position themselves as specialists. Generally, a market segment can be penetrated more rapidly and more deeply by concentrated firepower. Another unique characteristic of sales professionals is that they will have shown an ability to succeed in their target market segments—for example, manufacturing. Most sales professionals also manage to glean information from the most unusual sources to become fully informed. As a consequence of their research and target marketing, they become recognized experts in their field. Customers will come to them more than they need to seek out customers. Sales professionals will gain reputations around the marketplace. If you place a sales professional in a purely order-taking role, you are depriving him or her of opportunities to use the above skills. Conversely, if you place an order taker in a selling role, you could cause stress leading to fear and an inferiority complex, and probably lose potential sales.

It has been suggested that 90 percent of an order clerk's salary should be in the form of guaranteed pay and 10 percent should be based on performance. By contrast, a sales professional should receive no more than 20 percent as a retainer and 80 percent in incentives. In these hard times, you might try asking your sales people to contribute to overhead in exchange for 100 percent commission. It is one way to cut down any costs while you are building scope to increase your sales. Sales professionals should have no upper limit to their earning potential. There is no problem with the sales professional earning a lot more than the owner of the company.

Whatever sales system you adopt, it is important that staff members report to the manager or yourself weekly and fill out detailed reports—whom they visited, what was said, the required follow-up. You should review these every week and compare them with the previous week's. Ensure that every product is being sold at the standard gross or net profit margin. It is profit that keeps the business going, not turnover. Some sales professionals are quite clever about producing the turnover, but profit is hard to find. Ensure that your sales staff sell only to approved customers. Pay your commissions monthly; don't get behind—it is the quickest way to destroy staff morale. Have regular contests to add variety to the competitive spirit. For example, any sales professional introducing five new customers in a month could receive a dinner for two with accommodations at a local five-star hotel. These should be built into your budget and only claimable once the profit has been achieved.

Most sales professionals will have their own systems of control and recording, but it is very important that they share their systems with you. It is basically your customer and your product, and you need to know the mechanics of how your customer is being serviced. It is important to make sure that they keep diaries and manage their time efficiently. They should be proactive, rather than reactive, to the customer's requirements. Card systems must be maintained in duplicate so that the internal sales team has a record of recent promises, discounts, deals, or special arrangements with customers.

The sales professional's success should also be judged in terms of the journey, not just the destination. He or she should constantly be moved on to new areas that need to be developed. Financial consideration can be provided during this changeover period.

Sales professionals should be fully acquainted with their customers and their customers' financial positions, not only so that they can sell more effectively but so that you will be confident of getting paid. Particularly in a tough economic environment, it is important to sell but not to push too hard. Many a time, customer resistance is based on the knowledge that the customer cannot buy because the customer cannot afford to pay. And remember, there's no point in making a sale if you can't collect.

> **Case Study.** Charles is in the clothing manufacturing business, supplying mainly to retailers. He faces stiff competition and is vulnerable to the possibility of his customers going out of business. He has hit on a new idea to do with the value-added service concept. He offers a free computer service that analyzes the vital accounting and bookkeeping statistics of his customers' businesses. He sends these customers questionnaires, which they complete monthly, giving their vital sales figures, purchasing costs, lines they are carrying, turnover, number of customers, and so on. They also include their budgets. Charles gets all this information, compiles and consolidates it, and then sends back an analysis of how a customer is doing compared to the other users

of the system (anonymously, of course). Generally, people who are taking advantage of this service are interested in being more profitable. So, in locking his customers in to his service, he is helping them to become more profitable and because of this they are in turn able to purchase more of his products. It is also a means of monitoring how his customers are doing. In these tough economic times, he can identify which of his customers are getting into financial trouble. He can offer ways to help them and, if it looks like they are getting into financial trouble, he can withdraw from them in advance of being stuck with a bad debt.

Finally, make sure your sales professionals can accomplish the following:

- Ask for the order.
- Earn loyalty by empathizing with the customer at all times.
- Know the facts, not only about your business but about their customers.
- Know the correct title and position of the customer they are dealing with, and try to reach the decision maker as quickly as possible and approach him or her properly.
- Always show that they care about their customer's business as well as their own, and always try to judge the people they are selling to—whether they are aggressive, timid, apprehensive, and so on— and act accordingly.
- Develop the skill of listening.
- Always fulfill promises, follow up, document what they say they will do and do it on time, telling the customer in advance if they are unable to do it.
- Adopt good time management techniques.
- Adopt the KIS (Keep It Simple) principle.

- Are efficient and maintain neat work areas.
- Attend to

    Appearance. Look and feel comfortable. Wear the right clothes. Be groomed accordingly. Drive a reliable vehicle that suits the position.

    Equipment. Always have handy a spare pen and paper, an accurate watch, and some change for a telephone call or the parking meter.

    Card system. Have and use an efficient card system or computer diary. The card system should be clear, up to date, and full of facts about the customer, containing at least twenty pieces of information for each contact.

    Diary. Have and use a diary. A diary is the heart of a good salesperson's hardware and should be used throughout the day to make notes for later review and transferral to the card system or a notebook. Action notes should also be made in the diary for follow-up.

Diversification—Its Risks

With the freedom of running your own business comes the inevitable temptation to spread into new areas of endeavor. This is particularly the case for creative people, people with active, restless minds, people with the very enterprising traits that led them into their own business in the first place. But diversification can be a mistake: You might be better off sticking to what you know, the area in which you have experience, contacts, and technical know-how. You might want to, as the saying goes, "stick to your knitting." Part of the reason for having a mentor or an independent strategic planner on your board of directors is in fact to help you "stick to your knitting."

Resisting the urge to diversify often means persisting with a business activity that is downright boring. However, boredom often equates to cash flow, which equates to profits. It is common to see a business that is successful in one city expand into other states for the sake of expansion. But this duplicates overhead, communication costs, and travel and accommodation costs. It doesn't help in the overall objective of achieving profits. It is also common to see entrepreneurs make a lot of money out of property speculation and, suddenly thinking they are the greatest business managers on earth, move into manufacturing or some other area of business in which they have no expertise at all.

> **Case Study.** Darren ran a hardware business. He worked very hard, but didn't pay much attention to monthly figures, margins, and collecting his money. His wife was left to sort out the books and get things in order from time to time. After some years, Darren went for a trip to another city. There he discovered a warmer climate and, claiming that this meant a greater demand for his product and his marketing expertise, he proceeded to set up an interstate office. He traveled frequently between the two cities on the pretext of keeping an eye on the business, but failed to spend time with his new staff because he was more interested in his new social life. The new office business lost money from the start.
>
> Eventually Darren decided to close the interstate office and stop the waste. But he was unable to sublet the premises, so his $5,000 loss per month, although less than an initial $20,000, was still a substantial amount for a small business.

Of course, as you occasionally take stock of the environment in which you operate, this might suggest the desirability of moving into a different line. But, rather than stray from your company's known strengths, you should look at making greater use of them in a different way.

You may identify the need for a new product or service to market to your current customers, or for developing a new market for existing products. New fields may open themselves to you through the acquisition of other concerns or the purchasing of manufacturing licenses. If this is the case, take a close look at your resources, your property, your own skills, and your strengths and weaknesses. What plant, labor, and financing do you have available? Are they being used to their most profitable extent? Analyze sales patterns and estimate demand, both short and long term.

Research other possibilities. Beware of entering any high-technology market when introducing a new product. It is safer to rely on bread-and-butter lines unless you are fortunate enough to have the necessary technical expertise in-house. Again, aim at staying within the boundaries of your business's established strengths and the industry you know.

However, there are circumstances under which a business can diversify successfully. The most common opportunities are when profit or growth objectives cannot be achieved through the existing business; when the existing business is too dependent on one industry, market, or customer; when cash flow exceeds current requirements; when competition is depressing growth of profit margins; or when major customers decide to make the product themselves. It is certainly crucial to diversify your customer base, so that your financial viability is not dependent on anyone else's.

If you have decided to diversify for any of the above reasons, you must be prepared to raise large sums of money and, if necessary, to locate suitable venture partners. This involves a disciplined and far-reaching search for opportunities and includes surveys of past growth markets, new technologies, large or larger markets, firms of potential that are badly managed, profitable companies with a similar major shareholder, and existing synergy. (Synergy comes in various forms: sales synergy, in which products have common distribution outlets, administration, warehousing, or advertising; operating synergy, in which manufacturing plants can be combined to reduce overheads; and research and development synergy.)

Under appropriate circumstances, diversification can bring major benefits to small businesses by reducing dependency on a particular market, by equalizing sales in cyclical markets, or by offering opportunities in growth markets. The first step is to prepare a new or an amended business plan. But be warned: Diversification is risky.

Handling Success

Contrary to popular mythology, success in business brings its own set of problems and, therefore, requires careful management. Whereas sudden failure has a sobering effect, sudden success is inclined to give business owners a false sense of security. Yet, as you well know, bad times will follow good (how quickly, you won't know), and a flush period should be used to prepare for an inevitable dry spell.

Proper financial planning is the key. By keeping you in touch with the exact current status of your business, it will enable you to make accurate predictions about the immediate future and give you a broad picture of the longer term. Ideally, it will prepare you for any eventuality, positive or negative, and will enable you to anticipate rises and falls in cash flow.

When the good times do roll, your attitude is important. Don't let success go to your head. Continue to work for tomorrow, not for today. Persist with the hard jobs. Continue to lead by example. Don't employ excess staff or purchase or lease expensive equipment because of your success. Don't go out and squander your wealth on expensive cars or vacations. The debt will still be there when the cash flow has long since dried up. Remember the fundamental rule: Do what is best for yourself and your family first; then consider cash flow (even in good times); and last of all consider what is best for tax purposes. Stick to your business plan and listen to your advisers. So many business people from humble beginnings lose their sense of perspective at the first sign of substantial profits. They change their lifestyles dramatically, neglect their businesses, and then very quickly get into trouble. Don't be like them.

Build soundly and don't manipulate. Don't assume that if you succeed in one business area or product you will automatically succeed in another. By all means diversify your cash flow, but do it carefully.

Stick to your budget, every line of it. Always compare with the actual expenditures, particularly those in the personal area of travel, entertainment, and cash. Use profits gained in good times to provide for the not-so-good times or unforeseen disasters, or for expansion. The fundamental rule of putting aside 10 percent of your profit as spare cash for emergencies or company expansion is a good one. If you develop this habit during easy times, it will be firmly entrenched when things get difficult. Now is the time to make sound investments, but be sure to diversify them and maintain flexibility so that you can grow carefully and gently. Spread your investments among the various sectors—real estate, cash, stock, bonds, and so on—and ensure that each investment has a separate legal owner, all controlled by your family.

Now is also the time to improve your people skills through courses and seminars and to invest in staff training. Having built up the marketing and/or production side of the business, you should now concentrate on recruiting, managing, motivating, and retaining valued staff. People are the most important aspect of your growth. Practice delegation. Many businesses eventually fail or never realize their full potential because of their founders' inability to delegate and manage people. Use the luxury of financial stability to transfer some of the load onto your staff; if this causes problems you will have the resources to handle them. Delegation is too late when tough times have already set in.

Continually reassess your own strengths and weaknesses and, as your business grows, the strengths and weaknesses of your business. Diversify into other areas only if they capitalize on your strengths and overcome your weaknesses.

The more successful your business becomes, the more you should review and rewrite your business plan, and the greater the attention you should pay to the fundamentals. Fundamentals include setting personal financial goals and personal financial planning, analyzing your current financial position and your borrowing, retirement planning, training, good advice, budgeting and reporting, time management, and tax planning. In business, you must always expect the tide to turn; you must always plan for tomorrow by setting aside cash reserves and having available lines of credit.

PART THREE

STAYING THERE

7

PROTECTING YOURSELF AND YOUR BUSINESS

Most of the hard work in the life of a small business is devoted to *getting there* and to the managerial art of *being there*. The vital issue of *staying there* depends largely on protecting what has been achieved, personally as well as professionally.

Looking After Yourself

You know the theories about working for yourself: You have more free time; you are your own boss; you have flexible hours; and you have time to look after yourself. But how often is this really the case? There is an opportunity for some improved quality of life. You may be able to live closer to your work and you might get greater satisfaction from being a part of the enterprise for which you work. On the other hand, self-employment is also riskier. The greatest hazards include the illusion of indispensability, family pressure, not being able to lock the problems behind the office door at night, not taking a proper vacation, and lack of attention to exercise and diet. These can lead to ill health, an early death, or interpersonal problems. Tough economic times, in particular, take their toll on self-employed people.

All the above hazards can be minimized, if not eliminated, by time management and planning. Just as your business benefits from having a basic purpose, long- and short-term objectives, and adequate resources, so do you personally. People who plan their lives take into consideration their personal resources, capabilities, preferences, and limitations. They are, therefore, better able to recognize and seize opportunities as they come along.

It is just as important to know what kind of person has a disease as to know what disease the person has. In other words, mental and physical health are interdependent. You cannot eliminate worry altogether; but when you are well and rested, the worry assumes its true proportions instead of being magnified. Likewise, the right mental attitude contributes to good physical health and enables you to cope much more easily with business problems.

In recent years, much has been said and written about the health of business executives and the stress of modern business life. Perhaps the answer is simply the application of day-to-day common sense. Intelligent living habits do much to ensure the smooth functioning of your system. Food, rest, and exercise should be regulated and balanced—all things in moderation. Try to stay within 10 percent of your ideal body weight. Exercise is important for keeping toned and for relaxing, as well as for stimulating creative thought. Above all, maintain a positive attitude. It is easier said than done, but warding off depression is an important weapon against failure in adverse circumstances. Seek professional help if you feel unable to cope with the problems yourself.

Also, look after yourself materially. You should allow yourself enough money to maintain an appropriate standard of living and to guard against risks. Do a personal budget along the lines of your business budget, allowing for all your expenses and your vacations. Attend to all aspects of your personal financial planning; identify personal goals and objectives and plan your investments, borrowing, and budgeting. Make sure you have more money coming in than going out. Bring your will up to date, plan for retirement, and make sure you have adequate insurance against illness, against loss of income, and against death.

If you have dependents, make sure there is more than enough money to provide for them in the unfortunate event of your death. Allow for the payment of all bills and ensure that there is sufficient money to maintain the family's lifestyle and meet educational needs.

Above all, enjoy what you do for a living. At least a third of your life is spent at work. If it doesn't give you happiness and satisfaction, the other two-thirds are not much good to you.

Looking After Your Business

To many people, insurance is nothing more than a waste of money. An individual may well get away with such a careless attitude, but in business the range of potential disasters is so vast that insurance makes more sense than ever before. In tough times, the probability that those potential disasters will actually happen increases so significantly that a failure to insure against them might lead to financial suicide.

If you did not do so when first setting up, you should think seriously about covering your business for the following major contingency.

- Theft or damage of contents, including theft of cash
- Public, and possibly private, liability
- Professional liability
- Workers' compensation
- Loss of profit

- Damage to vehicles, premises, private cars, goods, and so forth
- Debtors' failure to pay
- Your own disability (perhaps most important of all)

Before looking into the details of different kinds of insurance coverage, you should identify the risks you face by carrying out a "risk audit." This involves a complete analysis of your business to see what dangers exist and what you can do about them. Obviously it is much better, wherever possible, to avoid risk by prevention. This can be done simply by being more careful, attending to dangerous equipment and slippery surfaces, making sure your employees are educated in safety regulations and procedures, and making sure they look after themselves. Make sure your premises have all appropriate fire safety equipment— fire extinguishers (for paper and electrical fires), first aid kits, and burglar alarms. Make sure tools and sharp objects are stored neatly and safely when not in use and that waste is removed regularly. Promptly repair any faulty buildings, equipment, motor vehicles, plumbing facilities, and electrical systems. All work should be carried out by qualified technicians.

If you have recently joined the ranks of the self-employed, your personal insurance position will warrant review. No longer is an employer in the wings waiting to pay your retirement or pension. When considering your own needs, don't forget your spouse and children if you are married. Family income benefits are not normally very expensive to set up and would make a huge difference in the event of a calamity. You should think seriously about arranging coverage on your directors' and partners' lives for the benefit of the business in the event of their early demise.

Additionally, you should have an ordinary life policy, preferably of the endowment type. This is one that pays out after a set number of years or in the event of death. If this is too expensive to maintain initially, take out term coverage that you will be able to convert into a whole-life policy when cash flow permits. Finally, consider the benefits of private health insurance.

Obviously, fire coverage should be considered to protect principal assets and consequential loss of profits. There is also public liability to cover your liability to third parties for personal injury or property damage. A number of other policies might be appropriate, depending on the type of industry you are in. These include contractor's risk, boiler explosion, plate glass, product liability, marine transit, personal accident and illness, electronic equipment, machinery breakdown, and "fidelity guaranteed" to protect you against employees embezzling or stealing goods or money. In line with modern business practices some insurers now offer package policies—for example, industrial, office, or farm packs.

You should read all your policy documents carefully to see what has been deleted and what is excluded, particularly when it comes to storm, rainwater, and flood damage.

Also beware of the danger of being underinsured. Under the terms of the "coinsurance" clause, the insurance company will cover you only for the proportion of the total for which you are insured. For example, if a person in a business insures goods worth $100,000 for only $50,000, and the entire stock is destroyed, $50,000 will be paid out and the business will lose out by $50,000. However, if only half the stock insured for $50,000 was destroyed, the insurance company would pay only $25,000. The rationale is that the destructive force—fire, for example—would not have been so selective as to have destroyed only the insured stock. The most common coinsurance ratio—that is, the proportion of total coverage that the insurance company will pay out regardless of your actual coverage, is 90 percent. This is quite generous, but there is no law saying that it has to be so.

Don't skimp on insurance. Deal only with first-class brokers or insurance companies with good reputations for prompt payment of claims. You should actively manage your insurance and not let any policies lapse. It is helpful to review all your insurance at the same time, on an annual or semiannual basis.

The Law: For and Against You

The law as it affects small business is complicated, detailed, and beyond the scope of this book. The law exists to protect you, but your own ignorance can make it work against you. With the help of your chosen lawyer or lawyers, you should educate yourself about the ins and outs of some or all of the following as they become relevant.

- Statute law
- Common law
- Contract law
- Consumer protection
- Copyright designs, trademarks, and trade names acts and laws
- Employer and employee laws
- Contracts of employment
- Leases and rental agreements
- Securities and Exchange Commission (SEC) requirements
- Regulations for businesses and use of premises

- Registrations, permits, licenses, or agencies
- Health requirements
- Electrical installation requirements

You must take personal responsibility for reading all legal documentation pertaining to your business. There are no safe shortcuts or compromises. The fine print may be boring and hard to understand, but you must tackle it so that no one else can be blamed for any misrepresentation. You must read legal documentation very carefully, even when you are signing a lease. Be aware that most legal documents having to do with renting, leasing, buying, or borrowing have personal guarantees in them. The personal guarantee, as discussed earlier, is the very shirt off your back and, wherever possible, you should avoid signing one. If there is no option, make sure that your liability is limited to a specific amount or to a specific facility and that any multiple guarantees are "several" rather than "joint and several." (The former means that any one party is liable only for his or her portion of the debt. The latter means that any one party can be held liable for the total debt in the event that the other parties are unable to pay.) Most banks have documents called "joint and several" guarantees. At the time when you sign them, there might be a line of credit of $100,000. When further accommodations are granted to the company, the debt position grows and the guarantee, because of its wording, picks it all up and passes it back to the guarantors in the way of liability. Generally, the banks want to be able to hold any one person liable for the whole amount.

If you resign your company directorship and/or sell out of a company, you should make sure you obtain a release from any guarantees you have signed. Under favorable circumstances, banks will usually release one director who is leaving the company, provided they get a guarantee from the new director who is coming in and provided he or she is financially viable. If the bank won't release you, at least notify the bank that you are exiting and that you will not be liable for any further credit extended to the company to which you have not given your express consent. That at least gives the bank notice that you are no longer there. A bank generally will give notice about extending further credit to a company in those circumstances; however, the bank can extend credit to the company on any terms it likes, and you are liable whether you know about it or otherwise. You could at least muster an argument against the bank that it ought not to rely on your guarantee to the extent of any further credit extended after the date on which you gave the bank notice that you exited.

If at all possible, avoid cross-collateralization. When a small business has a number of operating entities within a group—that is, perhaps two or three companies operating different facets of the business—there may be assets held in several of the entities and not just in one. If one of the companies is the borrowing entity, the banks may use very powerful documents to bring every company within the net so that each becomes a guarantor of the other.

A lawyer mentioned a recent case in which a company that is now in liquidation had a variety of loans from the bank, and certain properties were mortgaged to secure those loans. His client, who was a director of the company, tried to argue that a particular property secured a particular loan and no other. This produced adverse financial repercussions because some properties were worth more than the loans that they secured and some less. On the face of the documents, the court rejected the director's argument and lumped all properties together to cover all liabilities because the guarantee was worded "all monies."

Case Study. Peter went into the used car business. Although he was a very good salesman, he wasn't good at managing his business. He was good at talking to customers, but paid no attention to detail. He signed personal guarantees without really understanding the ramifications. Peter signed joint and several guarantees and cross-collateral guarantees for the various car lots that he developed as he went along. He had personal guarantees on the floor plan for his cars. He leased equipment. Things were going well when the economy was all right. But when things started to go bad, Peter found that he wasn't making enough sales, and the sales he was making were at vastly reduced prices so the gross profit was down. He had enough stock to pay his creditors, but he didn't have enough to pay the rent on the building or to cover the equipment that he had leased or the floor plan. Even though he thought he had protected himself and had his assets separated, he soon discovered the catastrophic effect of the documents he had signed. He hadn't read the fine print. He has since sworn that if anyone puts a pen in his hand, he will use it only to scratch his back.

Family property should be completely separate from the business. It needn't be owned by a separate legal entity altogether as long as whoever owns the property isn't going to be liable in any way to anybody as a result of the operations to the company.

Bankruptcy is fairly wide reaching and you would be foolish to hatch scams and schemes to dispose of assets. Ideas such as selling all your assets to a totally independent person may work, but they can just as easily be set aside.

At all times, avoid the legal mine field. If you are caught in this respect, you can only blame yourself. Either you didn't read the fine print, or you didn't pay enough attention to detail, or you didn't plan ahead. Address your problems—whether to do with partnerships, customers, employees, creditors, or whatever—as and when they occur; don't allow them to fester and grow out of proportion.

In this respect the Japanese seem to have it worked out: They have quite a lot of business schools and hardly any law firms.

Make an effort to resolve disputes before the need for legal action arises: Talk the issues through and come to an agreement, even if there is a cost involved. A far greater cost, without doubt, is that of getting embroiled in the legal system. This is quicksand for small businesses, and it is unknown territory—once you get in, you will have little chance of getting out unscathed. The only winner of the game is the legal system itself. The costs to you are time, cash, worry, and disruption of the stability of your personal and business life. If you do require the services of a lawyer, for example when planning a business agreement or trying to settle a dispute, gather all documentation and establish a legal framework yourself before making contact. Instruct the lawyer specifically in your requirements rather than asking for advice. Advice not only attracts a higher fee, but it also means that you do not own the decision that it prompts. Finally, remember that with lawyers you need a general practitioner as well as access to a number of specialists, just as you do for health care.

8

ON THE BRINK

Business failure is a fact of life during periods of recession, and its incidence is increasing. The real tragedy is that a high proportion of all bankruptcies could, and should, have been avoided.

Apart from the general problem of bad management, the main specific cause of small business collapse is the simple failure to keep proper records. As you have seen, business operators need to watch five key indicators to know how they are doing: the level of turnover, the level of debts owed at any time, the level of credits due or receivables, the value of stock, and the level of available bank credit. By tracking the movement of those five things from one period to the next, you can work out whether you are getting into trouble or whether you are staying profitable.

In the absence of proper records, business owners often don't prepare budgets, so they don't plan ahead. Or, if they do prepare budgets, they don't compare actual performance with the budget to find out how they are doing. If they fall short of the sales budget, they might look for the reasons; but if they exceed the sales budget, they often ignore the reasons. As you saw in Chapter 6, however, a better-than-budget result is frequently due to factors quite separate from those that were planned. The business might have picked up a very significant order from one sector of the economy, giving it better turnover and profitability for a particular quarter, but this might be a singular occurrence. In fact, the business might be going down, with the decline being masked by the windfall.

Perception is also a common problem. Because of their characteristic optimism, too many entrepreneurs refuse to accept that things are going badly. They have not worked for salaries or wages and gone home every day at five o'clock. They eat and sleep their businesses, and they have probably involved their families as well. They are too close to make an objective assessment of the situation. They don't want to recognize the danger signs because they can't accept that these probably reflect on their own management. A by-product of this is introspection—looking too closely at your business at the expense of knowing what is going on around you.

Making the Hard Decisions

Don't let bankruptcy creep up on you. Act to prevent it. Tough times call for hard decisions, and these cover the whole spectrum of the business plan, from the decision to get out in the field and spend more time with your customers to the decision to work more hours or perhaps even spend less time at home. It is hard to lay off staff or reduce their wages, to delay payment to creditors, to dare to go and sit in people's offices and collect your money, to upset people in the short term for the sake of long-term survival. It is hard to get rid of surplus equipment, replace a new car with a second-hand one, or get rid of surplus stock at a price lower than it is worth. Certainly, it is hard to cut your own wages and adopt a more moderate lifestyle. It is hard to go to your banker and ask for extended credit, to maintain tight cash control. All these are hard decisions; in tough times they crop up more frequently than usual and their effect is more critical.

Look at ways of minimizing waste. This should be second nature in all economic climates, not just when things are tough. If undertaken as a team effort, it can be quite a challenge. Obviously every business is different, and the following list of suggestions is offered as a starting point only. At best it will stimulate you to come up with your own ideas.

- Pay a car allowance rather than buy a new vehicle.
- Don't let your staff members fill their tanks on Fridays or Mondays with gas supplied by the company unless they have special approval.
- When possible, give products as a promotional tool rather than nondeductible gifts or cash.
- Constantly monitor your use of couriers compared with mail, facsimile, and phone. Indiscriminate use of couriers is expensive.
- Monitor the cost effectiveness of mobile telephones. Are they really essential for an organized sales professional or representative?
- Continually reappraise company cars and equipment supplied to staff.
- Invoice all samples, gifts, or products used internally against the relevant account to enable control and appraisal and to avoid abuse.
- If you have a large number of interstate suppliers, consider asking them to obtain toll-free telephone numbers. If they are not prepared to do so, suggest that they call you rather than you call them.
- Monitor freight alternatives. There are many different methods available: bus, rail, mail, independent

trucking, courier, and your own transport. Choices change with size, quantity, and style of goods. Watch how you categorize your deliveries, because some companies charge on mass, where weight would be much more competitive depending on the category of goods. Carefully check every invoice you receive from a freight company; they are renowned for promising one thing at the initial contract stage and delivering another at the invoice stage.

- If you use writing pads, turn them with the glued end toward you and write from the cut edge down, using a ruler to tear off only the piece you have used. The paper will go a lot further.

- Recycle wasted or obsolete photocopies by using the other side. Create a store of scrap paper from old files. Ask your banker for free scraps of pads or cut wastepaper into pads. It may sound petty, but watching the pennies means that the dollars will look after themselves.

- Recycle used envelopes by covering the old address with a stick-on label.

- Never throw out anything with a paper clip or butterfly clip still attached.

- Set a donation schedule at the beginning of the year. This avoids random donations by anyone on your staff or by yourself in a weak moment. Another idea is to offer charities stock at cost price rather than making a monetary donation.

- Check size and effectiveness of computer reports. Large, unnecessary reports are not user friendly, and they waste paper and equipment time as well as taking longer to read.

- Ask yourself if you really need packing slips. Can't your invoices also serve as statements? Sending out statements is an unnecessary cost that actually delays the payment of the invoice. It is common these days to eliminate the statement process and request payment against invoice.

Be tough, but don't be hasty. For example, think twice before slashing your marketing budget, no matter how tempting this might be. Tough times offer fertile ground for the enterprising marketer. While your competitors are retreating in their marketing efforts, you can be scooping up opportunities that they have let go. Rather than reduce spending on advertising during hard times, businesses can profit by at least maintaining their normal allowance. Using advertising to gain an edge over your competitors may be less expensive in real dollars in uncertain times than it is in good times, when more companies maintain a strong profile. Take advantage of the fact that many sellers of advertising space actually reduce their rates during bad times to attract customers. And if you still need to reduce advertising costs, rather than decide not to advertise at all, you might look at the possibility of doing your own. Any advertising undertaken in this climate must be very accurately targeted.

Also be careful if you are forced by tight cash flow requirements to lay off staff and pay out large lump sums. Make yourself aware of your legal obligations as an employer and provide some sort of counseling, whether internal or external, to the displaced personnel. (Reflecting the current economic climate, a new consulting industry has sprung up to assist displaced employees reestablish their careers and minimize the effects of terminations on individuals and organizations.) Adequate notice should be given in writing and at least in line with the frequency of payment. (If payment is monthly, give one month's notice or if it is weekly, give one week's notice). Quite often employers will make a payment in lieu of notice. The advantage of this is that it prevents the disgruntled employee from undermining the owner and upsetting clients. Explain that the termination is necessary to protect the jobs of the other staff and to enable the business to survive. Presuming it is the case, point out that you have applied the principle of "last in, first to go" as a matter of fairness.

Finally, don't sell assets that dramatically affect the immediate and long-term future productivity or profitability of the business. Whenever possible, don't sell real estate assets. Concentrate on selling those assets that are superfluous, nonproductive, and don't enhance your income. Try to hang on to your home because you can always borrow against it. Banks prefer "bricks and mortar" security like that.

Assessing the Situation

Once you have considered and made all the available hard decisions, you will be in a position to isolate problems that are specific to your business from those of the wider economic environment. If it is clear at this stage that you are unable comfortably to meet your commitments when they fall due and your business is sliding into trouble, act immediately. The sooner you act, the better the chance that you will be able to trade out of your problems with the support of your creditors and bankers.

Start by calling in a specialist accountant (see "Getting Good Advice," Chapter 6). As your own management skills will, at this stage, fairly or unfairly, be judged to be lacking, the accountant will be able to provide some sort of external credibility by objectively researching your financial affairs.

Once your accountant has investigated your situation in detail, he or she will prepare a report, including a detailed statement of position, and advise you on what to do next. The accountant will probably start by identifying where losses are occurring. Then he or she will make recommendations on how to reverse them, regain control over cash flow, and implement tighter credit control, particularly if debtors are not paying or are paying slowly, or if there are some potential bad debts. Your accountant will place controls over stock and production, making sure that stock is being turned over and there is no excess, and will obviously review and try to reduce overhead.

The scope of the accountant's report will vary according to the business, but obviously it will state what the immediate cash requirements are, what the latest asset and liability statement is, and what forecasts are available. Its purpose will be to establish whether your business is viable and to what extent, and to decide on a course of action.

The accountant's report will answer the following questions:

- What is the business predicament at the moment?
- How serious are the problems?
- Can the employees be paid?
- Is there adequate insurance to cover all the assets?
- Which creditors are essential to the continuation of the business?
- Are there any legal actions pending?
- Is there any action or threat of action to repossess any essential assets?

- If the premises are rented, what is the status of the lease?
- Is there any equipment that is subject to a usage-or-return agreement?
- Are there any forward supply commitments that can be canceled?
- Have any other things occurred that are peculiar to the business?
- Most importantly, what money is owed for taxes? (Keep the tax collector happy and paid up, because he or she is never sympathetic or slow to take legal action.)

This all takes time and makes demands on your stressed short-term memory, but your files should supply you with much of the information needed for this crucial document.

Establish your exact cash/bank position. Gather the facts, and list the monthly totals of receipts and payments for the last twelve months from the bank statements. If the cash book is up to date and the bank reconciliation completed, verify the figures you've gathered. List all unpaid creditors and isolate those who have to be paid to keep the doors open. Sort the rest according to commercial priority and descending dollar value.

Determine any forward order commitments, particularly overseas, and any bills payable. Review the debts listing. Test the age analysis (thirty, sixty, ninety days, and so on). Are slow paying debtors significant? Which of these are also good customers? Examine the correspondence file for incidents of complaints. They could signal a bad debt. Complete a physical stock inventory. Get opinions from stock clerks as to the slowness of stock. Note any items that could be disposed of. Obtain valuations for fixed and other assets. List all leasing, property rentals, and advertising commitments. Schedule the payments, particularly any periodical payments. Check the last company taxes paid. Verify your findings from payrolls. List employee vacation pay, leave of absence pay, and any deferred commissions. Determine the unpaid income tax position.

Your accountant will ask you for all the details about which assets are owned by whom and in whose name. Is there anything held in trust for third parties? Has anything been disposed of within the last few years?

Once you have established and documented your financial position in this way, some important questions must be asked to decide whether or not you can survive.

- What is the actual reason for the company's decline?
- What is the severity of the crisis?
- What is the attitude of the shareholders/bankers/creditors?
- What are the industry's characteristics—its products, its market, its competitors?
- What has been the company's traditional marketing strategy?
- What is the company's cost/price structure and its gross profit margin?
- What external events may assist or detract from recovery?

If the situation appears beyond redemption, your accountant will recommend that you consider closing down; if recovery seems possible, your accountant will recommend that you trade out of your current difficulties. The former solution is dealt with in Part Four. The latter will depend on the support of your creditors and lenders.

Surviving

Your first step on the road to recovery is to use all the information from your statement of position to redo the budget and cash flow forecasts, then ascertain who can be paid and how much. What do you have to collect and when? Develop a checklist. Does the business have any cash in it? What is the credit limit? Are there any unpaid checks? Are there any checks or cash to be banked? Is there any available cash just for banking?

The next thing to do is to find out what the business has to pay out over the next month. Estimate wages. Add up credits due. Assess your own drawings and resolve not to take so much out. Find out whether any other payments are to be made. Next, calculate how much money is to come in from cash sales, from payment by debtors, or any other income. Then decide how much money is needed to survive.

Good management is critical to the successful planning and implementation of a turnaround, particularly if you are to keep your staff and motivate them during this uncertain period. Bear in mind that the rescue will generally take longer than anticipated, and initial assessments will frequently underestimate the degree of change required.

The turnaround might be possible with your existing management structure, whether it be yourself or others, or it might require the appointment of a new chief executive or at least a new external, specialized accountant. The latter would certainly indicate your serious intentions and give some credibility to your rescue attempt. It may also give some confidence to your creditors and leave you to pay them back in good time. There is a general belief that the owner of a business who leads it into a serious financial crisis is probably not the one who will be able to lead it out of one. Obviously, the choice of chief executive or accountant is most important. You should look for people in your industry who have been successful before. If that person was available, he or she would take less time to settle in. Given the need to operate at a fast pace in the turnaround environment, where there is tremendous pressure to achieve results in the shortest possible time, a good manager from elsewhere in the industry may be less attractive than an outsider with successful turnaround experience; for example, the same person who prepared your initial investigation and statement of position.

Businesses that have experienced financial difficulties and have weak financial cash flow control systems will initially depend on gaining control over cash, preparing short-term forecasts, preparing detailed operating budgets, and reviewing all manufacturing and overhead expenditures. Effective systems in these areas need to be operational within weeks to establish control and direction.

Generally, businesses in severe financial crisis will need to look at recovery as a process consisting of two stages, whose order cannot be reversed. The first stage entails contracting your business back to a profitable cell. The second is to move toward growth-orientated strategies to build a sustained recovery.

In a financial crisis, the ideal action is often surgical in nature. Your business may withdraw from entire areas—by closure, divesting, or sale, and by limitation of product lines and/or customers that are unprofitable or where return on investment is poor. This cuts your operation back to its core so it can be profitable again.

Once your core business is reestablished, issues such as the pricing policy can be looked at again, and perhaps you can increase prices. It becomes critical to understand the competitive situation and price elasticity or demand for major product categories. Many small businesses underprice themselves. They are surprised to discover that even when they increase their prices, sometimes dramatically, they don't lose customers but in fact gain them. Elasticity means that, theoretically, if the price of your product goes up, demand will go down. However, an inelastic product is one where the price goes up but the product demand also goes up.

More attention should be paid to providing your existing customers with a total and proper service, ideally resulting in an improved selling effort, and to concentrating on those customers who will generate most of the profit.

A company in financial crisis will seek to return to profitability through reduction of costs, but it also needs to generate cash. Therefore, one of the strategies in the early days of the survival plan is to identify which assets are surplus and which assets are going to be necessary for the future profitability of the business. Sell the surplus to gain some cash.

An asset reduction strategy could include the following tactics:

- Eliminating product lines that are unprofitable or unnecessary.
- Selling subsidiaries or branches that do not meet profitable requirements or fit the company's refocused product market objectives.
- Selling underutilized or surplus fixed assets.
- Selling and leasing back land, buildings, and/or plant.
- Reducing working capital requirements by improving inventory.
- Reducing stock.

- Collecting your money more quickly and having fewer debtors.

Obviously, cutting back costs is most important. This could be done through repurchasing, buying more cheaply, or finding alternative sources to buy from. It could also come from better use of materials and by substituting materials.

Keep your staff on your side during these difficult times—reassure them, be honest with them, talk openly with them—because you will need them to help you out of your difficulties.

Unilateral thinking is required. Once all the costs have been cut back to a minimum and you have your core business profitable again, it may be a wise idea to protect yourself in the future by growing through acquisition of another company. You need to be very careful in this area, though.

Alternatively, the accountant's report may have revealed the need for an initial injection of funds. Therefore, new shareholders or joint venture partners may be sought to provide necessary capital to bring the business back to profitability. If this is not desirable, you might consider the possibility of finding an "angel," or someone who will buy your business from you at a reasonable price rather than becoming a partner. This again revolves around preparing a business plan and making sure the presentation is honest.

Normally, businesses in financial crisis have borrowed too much. This can have a crippling effect, particularly when interest rates are high. Debt restructuring and other financial strategies can form part of the overall rescue package. For example, the use of asset reduction strategies can assist in the reduction of borrowing levels. The success of any debt restructuring would depend on the new management's ability to convince financiers and other interested parties and creditors that the appropriate rescue plan has been put into action and the prospect of recovery is sound.

Here are some other ideas.

- Change your financial backers. (Often if a company has gone through a difficult period, it tends to lose credibility with existing lenders. Coupled with the new top management and the development of a recovery plan, it may be advantageous to consider an alternative source of funds.)

- Consolidate funding. (The company in a crisis will often have a proliferation of funding agreements with a number of different lenders. In order to reduce the overall cost, you might be wiser to convert short-term to longer term debt, to include current outstanding interest in the new loan, and to arrange for sale and lease-back of property and equipment.)

- Raise additional loans or convert existing loans to equity.

- Raise additional capital.

- If possible, obtain financial assistance from government agencies (highly unlikely in tough times).

Above all, it is important to keep everyone informed, particularly your banker and creditors, and be honest. Of course, this should be happening anyway. But it is particularly important when you are reading the danger signs and discover that your business is in trouble. Understand that your banker and your creditors don't want to lose you; they want to continue their business with you because you are their customer. If you get into trouble you will jeopardize not only the money you owe them but also future profits in terms of interest or future trading with your creditors.

To sum up, the action plan for a business staging a recovery is as follows:

- Divest yourself of surplus stock. Convert it into cash, or bail your way out of assets that have limited economic use. This includes personal assets. Perhaps the travel trailer that you haven't used for years can be traded in for a utility truck or a facsimile machine that would be useful in your business.

- Analyze what stock sells and in what quantities. Too much stock costs money. Too little stock loses money. Stock control is critical.

- Look at restructuring your loan portfolio and your lines of credit before the crunch really hits you. Ensure that you have adequate cash to draw on. Investigate how you are using your assets as security. Banks love nothing better than to have a small advance against a property with substantial worth. Most properties, including your house, can be mortgaged to about 80 percent of their value. Attempt to get larger unsecured lines of credit, such as credit cards with higher limits. Consider discretionary, unsecured, flexible lines of credit—rainy-day money that you may never need but that is in place when you do. The worst time to look for money is when you need it the most.

- Reduce staff numbers. Let go of those who do not contribute directly to the money-making function of the business. Retain your good people. You might have to be ruthless—if not, you could jeopardize the jobs of *all* your employees.

- Review all your overhead expenditures. Get rid of those that are not producing an economic return. Subscriptions to the local health club are fine in good times, but are questionable in the belt-tightening period. Look at tightening up capital expenditure. Reassess your spending priorities.

- Collect from your debtors. Review office procedures for the collection of cash, particularly debts. While ordering goods and services, examine the credit worthiness of your customers. Review the cost of producing goods and services that you sell. Look for cost savings. Look for assistance from your suppliers; they might agree to a slightly longer payment period. After all, they have a vested interest in your survival. Above all, look for the right price for the right goods and services from suppliers who are likely to weather the storm themselves.

- Get back to the basics of the business. Stick to what you know best. Identify your core products or services; identify your market strengths. Examine your competitors and their efforts to cope with tougher times. Conserve cash wherever and whenever you can. If necessary, extend existing leasing terms to defer large pay-outs of unproductive cash.

- Look after and service your customers.

PART FOUR

GETTING OUT

9

INSOLVENCY

I f your ailing business appears to be insolvent and all bids to save it have failed, you must consider your final options, some of which will enable you to stay in business.

Available Options

There are various types of insolvency administrations. You will need to consult a specialist lawyer and/or accountant about which one is appropriate for your circumstances.

A *Chapter 11* is an arrangement whereby the company's creditors agree to a moratorium on their debts to enable the company to continue to trade. This should never be undertaken without expert advice and assistance. In some cases, to give creditors confidence to accept an arrangement, a manager may be appointed to oversee the operations of the company and report on its performance. A formal Chapter 11 is one approved by the creditors and the court. Obtaining the necessary approval can be expensive and time consuming. An informal arrangement can be made, provided *all* creditors agree. This operates as a contract between all the creditors and the company. Unless all creditors are parties to the contract, an uncooperative creditor who is not a party could proceed to close down the company and this would, of course, unravel the scheme.

In *receivership* a receiver or receiver-manager is usually appointed by a secured creditor with control over some or all of the company's assets. The receiver-manager may or may not have the power to carry on the business of the company.

If you have acted early in recognizing trouble and appointing a receiver to take over from your investigating accountant, your business might gain much-needed breathing space to work out its difficulties. In this sense, the receiver is more like a doctor tending a sick patient than an undertaker preparing a body for burial. The time can be used to investigate the company's operations and to develop a business plan that takes it back to being a going concern. This may involve selling off unprofitable parts of the business or introducing equity. If you apply to the court yourself for the appointment of a receiver, you might have a better chance of obtaining a moratorium on payments to creditors.

When a receiver is appointed, he or she will carry out an investigation to ascertain the company's real position. The receiver will then place appropriate controls over all the key aspects of the business, including ordering systems, accounting systems, payment systems, cash receipts, and banking and stock. If the business is to continue as a going concern, the receiver will develop budgets with a view to survival. A receiver will be reluctant to continue trading in a company unless the outcome is reasonably certain.

Being in receivership is a new and worrisome experience for many company owners, and also for customers and suppliers, particularly if the business depends on continuous supply. The receiver will try to reestablish the confidence of the company's customers and suppliers, and to reassure them of eventual payment for any goods and services provided during the course of the receivership. The directors of a company in receivership have only limited powers and must observe certain statutory obligations. Responsibility for the day-to-day running of the business lies with the receiver, who may choose to dispense with the services of the directors.

Liquidation is the last step that precedes the dissolution of a company. A liquidator appointed to a company is charged with the orderly sale of its assets and the distribution of the proceeds to creditors and, if there is any surplus, to shareholders. The liquidator's powers include carrying on the business of the company, but only insofar as that is necessary to ultimately close down the company.

Under a *formal bankruptcy* (voluntary or involuntary), all divisible property becomes the property of the official trustee. Under this arrangement you may not lose all your property. The debtor is entitled to retain sufficient personal income, family allowances, and pensions as are necessary for support: beds, personal items of clothing, tools of trade up to a certain amount, and so on. The role of the trustee is to gather the divisible property of the debtor, to liquidate that property, and to divide the proceeds among the creditors according to priority set down by the law.

You may be able to make an *arrangement outside bankruptcy*, whereby creditors agree to accept either a once-and-for-all payment of a lesser sum in full satisfaction of all liabilities, or periodic payments. Creditors are unlikely to accept less than the full amount of their debts unless they are satisfied that there are no available assets or income that would give them a better return. They need to be convinced that they would not fare better under a formal bankruptcy. How you win their support will vary according to your personal circumstances. Sometimes a monetary contribution by a third party, such as a member of your family, over and above what you are able to provide for yourself, may be sufficient to convince the creditors that you have done your best.

The main advantages of an arrangement outside bankruptcy are

- It doesn't carry the stigma of bankruptcy.
- Your creditors may not have access to property that you acquired after entering into the arrangement.
- Your future income is usually protected.
- There are fewer potential criminal liabilities than in the case of formal bankruptcy.
- Provided you can win the support of your creditors, an arrangement may be made that is more suitable to your personal circumstances.

There are also distinct advantages for your creditors.

- They are likely to fare better under the arrangement than in a formal bankruptcy, particularly if the arrangement involves the continuity of your business.
- Generally the cost of the administration of the arrangement is less than in formal bankruptcy.

The law in relation to bankruptcy and other arrangements is very complex. Before you contemplate any insolvency administration, make sure that you obtain advice from a specialist.

Legal Obligations

Once your business has collapsed, there is very little you can do to alter the course of events, other than superficially minimizing your exposure to ruin by being aware of your legal obligations.

Corporation law imposes clear legal responsibilities on directors, and the courts are only too willing to enforce these. If you are in any doubt about your obligations as a director, or about the financial condition of your company, you should obtain appropriate expert legal and accounting advice at the earliest opportunity.

In desperate times, otherwise honorable people might be pushed by the sheer stress of it all to consider immoral, unethical, or downright illegal escapes. Guard against this temptation and make sure you emerge with your integrity intact; it may well be all you have left.

10

STARTING AGAIN

There is no doubt that American business is facing some formidable challenges. Things will continue to be difficult in many sectors of business, and in some—for example, the building and related industries—more than others. Almost everyone is affected. But people today are still not as bad off as people were during the Depression. Business people who survived that time know what it is like to cut costs, run on very minimal overhead, and continue operating; or to face up to the inevitability of having to shut down a business. They know more than anyone else that hard times require personal sacrifice. Follow their example: *Never look back, except to learn.*

Someone once said that it is when you are in the midst of a business failure that you should write down the lessons you have learned, and that you should keep this permanent record to read weekly for the rest of your life so that you understand it fully and reapply it. Most of this book deals with the basic tenets of going into business, being there, and staying there. The final part deals with getting out. This brief chapter addresses the optimistic subject of starting again. However, despite all that is written here, nothing will be as real and convincing as your own list of lessons learned from direct involvement. Only that list will be marked with the personal efforts and experiences that make every business endeavor a rich and—even in the wake of failure—rewarding one. The best intentions and all the research in the world can never prepare you for all contingencies. Having faced them once, however, you are certainly forewarned.

> **Case Study.** Martin was, by his own admission, very crea-
> tive. He didn't have an eye for detail, so although he could
> pull projects and people together, he could not follow them
> through. Martin seemed to get bored easily. During the
> early part of his career he was in printing. He had no trouble
> finding clients. The equipment, though heavily financed,
> was being paid for comfortably, and he was able to afford
> a fairly ambitious lifestyle. Things continued to grow. He
> put on more staff before he needed them, and soon he was
> employing fifty people. He didn't pay much attention to
> budgets. He didn't like meetings. His accountants and fi-
> nancial controllers were not able to control him. He was
> looking at tapping the overseas market.
>
> Then came the economic decline. Martin found him-
> self with high debts, high interest payments on leases, and
> customers who were in trouble and couldn't pay him. He
> had excessive overhead, and he had committed himself to
> extensive leased premises and a number of personal guar-
> antees. Things looked fairly grim.
>
> Then Martin decided to sit down and learn some les-
> sons. He didn't feel sorry for himself like so many people
> do when they get themselves into financial trouble. He
> didn't go around blaming other people. He identified a
> number of weaknesses in the way he had conducted his
> business. He had not paid enough attention to detail. He
> had not spent enough time with his employees. He then set
> about reducing his overhead, maintaining collectible cash
> flow from selling printing at a profit, reducing his lifestyle
> dramatically, cutting his own allowances, not spending
> money unless absolutely necessary, identifying those cus-
> tomers who would pay on time, and getting cash payments
> where possible. He dramatically reduced the size of his
> business.
>
> Martin managed to save his business. The only thing
> that was hurt was his ego, but he never felt sorry for himself.
> He only looked back to learn.

A business collapse can be a cathartic experience for you. While the pain and the hardship are still fresh, you have a perfect opportunity to refocus your priorities in life, to reevaluate the fundamentals. This time offers you a forced reassessment of whether you should be in business for yourself or whether you are better off being employed by someone else. Sure, you have failed, but what matters is what you are going to do about it. There is no virtue in self-pity; you will only lose the respect of all those around you—not only your loved ones but also your business contacts. As the saying goes, "Tough times come and go, but tough people last." Above all, try to maintain your pride and integrity, to be honest with everybody. If it is known that you have been honest all along and that you have done the best you possibly could under the circumstances, you will not be judged harshly and plenty of people will still want to deal with you.

Don't waste the experience; use it to start all over again. Begin by reading this book once more. Develop another business plan. Do your market research again. Through all this you might have developed some new skills, or even a new product. Many a successful entrepreneur has emerged from the ashes of a failed business. There is no shame in adding yourself to the list. Despite the tough current economic environment, there are enormous opportunities to start from scratch or to take over, merge, or develop businesses. Scan the "For Sale" columns; talk to your accountant; read the newspapers; keep your eyes and your imagination open. Now is the time for getting started, not for giving up. The collapse of one business is not the end of the world. It is the perfect recipe for the beginning of another, and the chance to make this business more prosperous than the last.

APPENDIX A: FINANCIAL STATEMENTS

The following is an analysis of the connections between the three financial statements on page 166.

Sales Revenue → Debts

The balance in the Sales Revenue account is the sum of all sales made during the year. Assume that the company made all its sales on credit. The amount owed to the company (receivables) is immediately recorded in Debts when each sale is made. Later, when customers pay their debts, the cash account is increased and Debts is decreased. The balance in Debts is the amount of uncollected sales at the end of the year.

Of interest to the manager, creditors, and investors alike is the average time taken to turn receivables into cash. The point is that the average sales credit period (ASCP) determines the size of debts relative to annual sales revenue. The longer the ASCP the larger the debts. Using information in financial statements, you can determine the ASCP as follows:

52 weeks divided by $\dfrac{\$4{,}212{,}000 \text{ (sales revenue)}}{\$486{,}000 \text{ (debts)}}$ = 6 weeks

Hence, at year-end, six weeks of the company's sales are still uncollected.

If the manager considers six weeks to be too long an ASCP, he or she can take certain steps to shorten it. If the company's ASCP had been only five weeks, the debts would have been $81,000 less, and the company would have collected $81,000 more in cash. At 10 percent interest on its borrowing, the company would have saved $8,100 before tax.

Cost of Goods Sold ← → Inventory

The cost of goods sold is deducted from the sales revenue to determine the gross profit. Inventory is the amount of stock held at the end of the financial year and is shown in the balance sheet as an asset. Of interest to the manager, creditors, and investors is how long the company holds an average item of stock before it is sold. The stock turnover ratio is most meaningful when it is used to determine the number of weeks it takes to sell stock. Using information in the financial statements, you can determine the average inventory holding period (AIHP) as follows

$$52 \text{ weeks divided by } \frac{\$2,808,000 \text{ (cost of goods sold)}}{\$702,000 \text{ (inventory)}} = 13 \text{ weeks}$$

The AIHP determines the size of inventory relative to annual cost of goods sold. The longer the holding period, the larger the inventory. If the holding period is longer than necessary, too much capital is tied up in inventory or there is too much cash in inventory and not enough in the bank.

If the company could reduce its AIHP from thirteen weeks to eleven, $108,000 capital would be saved ($54,000 cost of goods sold per week × 2). However, the AIHP should not be so low that goods are not available as needed to make sales. The cost of carrying inventory has to be balanced against the profit opportunities lost by not having the products in stock.

Inventory → Credits

When stock is purchased on credit, the liability for the amount of goods bought is recorded in Credits and the cost is recorded in Inventory.

Some purchases are paid for promptly, while others are not paid for two months or so. Based on its payments experience and policies, a business can determine the average credit period it waits before paying for its stock purchases. In this example, the average credit period is

$$52 \text{ weeks divided by } \frac{\$2,808,000 \text{ (cost of goods sold)}}{\$216,000 \text{ (credits)}} = 4 \text{ weeks}$$

Sometimes the amount of credits may be higher than normal when large purchases of stock are made just prior to year end or payment of bills is deliberately slowed down to conserve cash.

Operating Expenses → Credits

Operating Expenses includes all expenses of running the business except for depreciation, which is shown separately. Some operating expenses are recorded before they are paid—for example, electricity or telephone bills received but not paid until the new financial year. Generally, the credit terms of these creditors are not long. In this example, the average credit period of the company's unpaid operating expenses is:

$$52 \text{ weeks divided by } \frac{\$936,000 \text{ (operating expenses)}}{\$54,000 \text{ (credits)}} = 3 \text{ weeks}$$

Operating Expenses → Accrued Expenses (Payable)

Accrued Expenses would include such items as accumulated sick or annual leave pay, unpaid sales commission, part of annual rates and taxes or telephone costs that should be charged to this year but are not yet billed to the company. In this example, the average credit period of the company's accrued expenses is

$$52 \text{ weeks divided by } \frac{\$936,000 \text{ (operating expenses)}}{\$108,000 \text{ (accrued expenses)}} = 6 \text{ weeks}$$

It will be seen that a total of nine weeks' operating expenses are unpaid at year end (three weeks' credits and six weeks' accrued expenses). This relieved the company of a cash pay-out of $162,000 ($54,000 credits plus $108,000 accrued expenses).

If the company could have stretched the average credit period from nine weeks to eleven, it could have avoided an additional $36,000 of cash disbursements ($18,000 average weekly operating expenses × 2). In other words, credits and accrued expenses resulting from operating expenses have a significant impact on cash flow.

Operating Expenses → Prepaid Expenses

Certain operating costs are paid in advance and not charged against revenue until later. They are initially recorded as prepaid expenses, which is an asset account, and each month a portion is transferred out of the Prepaid Expenses and recorded in expense.

In this example, the company's prepaid expenses were equivalent to five weeks of its annual operating expenses:

$$52 \text{ weeks divided by} \quad \frac{\$936,000 \text{ (operating expenses)}}{\$90,000 \text{ (prepaid expenses)}} = 5 \text{ weeks}$$

If the manager could have reduced these prepayments from five weeks to three, prepaid expenses would have been only \$54,000, reducing the demand on cash by \$36,000. But, if prepayments had been seven weeks instead of five, the cash demand would have been \$36,000 more.

Property, Plant, and Equipment → Depreciation → Accumulated Depreciation

The company owns desks, display cabinets, a computer system, various machines and tools, and so on, which are lumped together and recorded in one account called Machinery, Equipment, Furniture, and Fixtures. These assets have a limited life span and are depreciated over each future year of expected use to the business.

In this example the company has assumed an average life of four years and depreciation is computed as follows:

$$\frac{\$464,000 \text{ machinery, equipment, furniture, and fixtures}}{4 \text{ years of useful life estimate}} = \$116,000 \text{ per year}$$

The amount of depreciation is not recorded as a decrease in the Assets account directly. Instead, it is added to the Accumulated Depreciation account, and the balance of this account is deducted from the original cost of the assets.

It should be kept in mind that if the useful life estimate is too short, depreciation expense each year is too high.

Interest Expense → Accrued Expenses (Payable)

Interest is a financial cost as opposed to an operating cost. Interest is charged each day for the use of borrowed money and is usually paid quarterly or half-yearly. On both short- and long-term loans there is a delay in paying interest, but the interest expense should be recorded for all days of the loan period. Any unpaid interest at the end of the accountancy period is recorded in Accrued Expenses, which is a liability account.

Here, nine weeks' interest is unpaid at year-end.

$$52 \text{ weeks divided by } \frac{\$52,000 \text{ (interest expense)}}{\$9,000 \text{ (accrued interest)}} = 9 \text{ weeks}$$

Income Tax Expense → Income Tax Payable

A taxation liability is incurred by companies that earn profits, including capital gains. This is provided for in the balance sheet and expensed in the profit and loss statement in the year in which the profit is earned.

Net Income (Profit) → Retained Earnings

Net income is the final profit after deducting all expenses from the sales revenue. Retained earnings is the amount of net income earned and retained in the business. Dividends are recorded as decreases in retained earnings.

In the example, no dividends were paid to shareholders, and the entire net income of $150,000 was retained in the business.

Retained Earnings keeps track of how much shareholders' equity was earned and retained in the business and is shown in the balance sheet separately from capital invested by shareholders (Paid-up Capital).

APPENDIX B: WHERE TO GO FOR HELP

Agencies

Chambers of Commerce

Services vary among chambers but may include advice, support, workshops or seminars, local business news, and other services specifically for small businesses.

Local chambers are usually a good source for demographic/economic data and statistics on the labor force, transportation/traffic, market characteristics, and other data pertinent to business location decisions.

Libraries

Check to see if any public libraries have business library branches or sections; larger metropolises generally do. Also, check major universities in your vicinity to see if they possess affiliated business libraries.

Local Planning Departments

Source of information on zoning and future development locations. See the government section of your phone book for address and phone of the local office.

U.S. Small Business Administration (SBA)

1414 L Street, N.W.
Washington, D.C. 20416

The SBA is the primary source of federal governmental assistance for small businesses. In addition to providing financing for many small businesses, it provides a number of services for free or at a small cost. SBA regional offices routinely conduct free or low-cost small business workshops. The SBA also offers many helpful publications.

The SBA offers the following hotlines:

SBA Answer Desk (800-8-ASK-SBA or 800-827-5722)

Recorded information on the following topics:

1. Starting your own business
2. Financing your business
3. Counseling and training
4. SBA services and local assistance
5. Minority small business
6. Veteran's affairs
7. Women's business ownership
8. International trade
9. Procurement assistance

SBA ON-Line (800-859-INFO if you use a 2400 baud modem or 800-697-INFO if you use a 9600 baud modem)

A national electronic bulletin board service that provides an overview of SBA information including the following:

- Information on SBA's programs
- National calendar of events
- Information on loans and financial management

Environmental Protection Agency (EPA) Small Business Ombudsman (800-424-5888)

Provides information about complying with EPA regulations and offers help with disputes.

*Export/Import Bank's Automated Information System
Small Business Hotline (800-424-5201)*

Specialized service to small exporters about doing business abroad.

Other SBA Offices

SBA Field Offices—See your phone book's government section for address and phone number of your local office.

SCORE (Service Corp of Retired Executives) (800-827-5722)
P.O. Box 15434
Fort Worth, Texas 76119

Retired experienced business executives offer their expertise and services to entrepreneurs through SBA's SCORE, which charges for out-of-pocket expenses but not for the consultant's time.

Associations

National Association for the Self-Employed (800-232-6273)

2121 Precinct Line Road
Hurst, Texas 76054

Nonprofit organization with membership dues of $72 annually. Conducts educational programs, offers group discounts for business and travel services, and sponsors charitable projects.

National Business Association (NBA) (800-456-0440)

Membership organization offering business assistance.

Trade Associations

See *Encyclopedia of Associations* (Gale Research) to find the address and phone number of the trade association for your industry.

Magazines

Entrepreneur (714-261-2325)

How-to articles and features on successful entrepreneurs are targeted to service, retail, and manufacturing businesses.

Forbes (800-888-9896)

A financial magazine that delivers articles about the richest people, mutual funds, prosperous companies, and other interesting financial information.

Fortune (800-621-8000)

Fortune is quoted more frequently than any other business magazine. Issues put you inside the mind of management, reveal business coups and catastrophes, deals of the year, America's most admired corporations, and much more.

Inc., The Magazine for Growing Companies (800-234-0999)

Their subtitle says it all. Articles of interest to small business and interviews with successful entrepreneurs.

Success (800-234-7324)

Includes articles on running a successful business, obtaining venture capital, effective selling, office automation, and how to manage one's company for growth.

Other

AT&T Toll-free 800 Numbers, Consumer and Business Telephone Directories

Toll-free directory contains alphabetical listings of businesses, organizations, and government agencies with toll-free 800 numbers. Business directories list all local organizations and businesses with phone service.

SUGGESTED READINGS

Burstiner, Irving. *Small Business Handbook*. New York: Prentice-Hall, 1989.

Gibson, Bill. *Boost Your Business in Any Economy*. Berkeley, CA: Ten Speed Press, 1993.

Hancock, William. *Small Business Legal Advisor*. New York: McGraw-Hill, 1986.

J.K. Lasser Tax Institute Staff. *How to Run a Small Business*. New York: McGraw-Hill Book Company, 1989.

Kuriloff, Arthur and John M. Hemphill, Jr. *Starting and Managing the Small Business, 2/e*. New York: McGraw-Hill Book Company, 1989.

McCormack, Mark. *What They Don't Teach You at Harvard Business School*. New York: Bantam, 1986.

Mucciolo, Louis. *Small Business: Look Before You Leap; a Catalog of Sources of Information to Help You Start & Manage Your Own Small Business, 2/e*. New York: Prentice-Hall, 1981.

INDEX